Dedication

To my mother, Jean Agey Denison
who made it all possible

The Great American Songbook

Stories of the Standards

by
Chuck Denison

Robert D. Reed Publishers • Bandon, OR

Robert D. Reed Publishers
P.O. Box 1992
Bandon, OR 97411
Phone: 541-347-9882 • Fax: -9883
E-mail: 4bobreed@msn.com
web site: www.rdrpublishers.com

Typesetter: Barbara Kruger
Cover Designer: Grant Prescott

ISBN 1-931741-42-5

Library of Congress Control Number 2003116296

Manufactured, typeset and printed in the United States of America

Contents

Personalities
Irrepressible Genius

"A person possesses talent; genius possesses the person." Isaac Stern made a distinction between talent and genius. In real experience, that line may be hard to draw. This is a book about songwriters, lyricists and composers taking talent into the atmosphere of immortality. Each personality featured has been accused of genius. And each is guilty. Still, there are the undeniable few, the towering Titans that make it look easy.

A generation may only get one Mozart. But the phenomenon that so baffled Salieri, in Mozart's time, continues to bewitch us. Now and then there appears, from nowhere, a talent so developed, so original, it changes the whole game. This kind of brilliance simply cannot be held down or hidden.

From now on, for example, everyone who plays a saxophone must deal with Charlie Parker. He changed everything. Each of the personalities described in this section changed the game forever. These were the possessed ones. They did not live easy lives; they were not always happy people. But their genius drove them to new discoveries. And the world followed.

Someone to Watch Over Me

George and Ira Gershwin

George Gershwin was twelve when the family bought a used piano. Older brother Ira was looking forward to piano lessons. He was the "good one." He read. He went to school. He did not skip school to wander the streets of New York, looking for trouble. Surely he would make a disciplined student of piano. Mother Rose saved money out of the weekly check, until the piano arrived. Everybody remembers the day. A crane hauled the stand-up piano to a window of the Gershwin's second floor tenement. Family and friends muscled the instrument into place, and little George sat down.

George was trouble. He was already known through the East Side immigrant neighborhood. He was bright and bored. Rose predicted he would become a "hoodlum" and spend his adult life in jail. Then he sat down. Now, Ira was supposed to become the family musician, playing nice, dignified music in the parlor. The entire family was dumbfounded when precocious George began to play. It made no sense—where had he learned? He not only played, he played well. He played very well! How? He had been experimenting here and there, he explained, as he played popular songs and classical themes. George, it was decided, would be the family musician.

By age fifteen, George was employed as a song plugger, pounding a piano in Tin Pan Alley, and cutting piano rolls. The following year he changed his name, from Gersh–vin to Gersh–win, and the legend began. Within the year his songs were being interpolated into Broadway shows. From there, the leap to writing his own show came easily to a genius as enormous as Gershwin's.

The musical scene was in a creative foment throughout the Nineteen Twenties. French Impressionists like Debussy and Ravel, influenced by the new perceptions of the visual artists, were stretching the rules of tonality and formal composition. In America, Jazz was establishing itself as a popular trend and a serious art form in its own right. Only George Gershwin managed to straddle these two worlds, and contribute significantly to both. His *Rhapsody in Blue, Concerto in F, An American in Paris* and other symphonic works apply the blues scales and swing rhythms of Jazz to the classical tradition. While his output of popular and show tunes is simply staggering, Gershwin created much of the subsequent musical vocabulary of Jazz, including penning the ubiquitous *Rhythm Changes (I've Got Rhythm)*.

Historian Osbert Sitwell wrote, "The hundreds of songs and dances George Gershwin wrote were altogether typical in their audacity of the age that gave them birth; the Twenties lived and expired to his ingenious tunes, so expert of their kind...no chronicle of the epoch could fail to mention them and their pervasive influence."

Gershwin lived his life with infamous intensity. He was usually seen smoking a cigar and playing a piano. He courted several loves, often simultaneously, proposed frequently, and never married. He wrote for Tin Pan Alley, Broadway, Carnegie Hall and Hollywood. His brother Ira, sedate, literary and contemplative, was both his confidante and lyricist. While George worked with other writers, and Ira wrote for other composers, their best work was done together.

By their middle twenties, the brothers were the center of a small circle of writers, composers, actors and musicians that were creating the music for the decade. Yip Harburg remembers, "We got together every night, often at the Gershwins, where there were two pianos and we could play everything we had written that week...there was a real camaraderie."

Gershwin was usually in love—with someone. Occasionally it was with more than one someone. In 1925 George was in love with Kay Swift. She began to work with him as a "second piano." She would score some of his melodies; she rehearsed musicians and singers and dancers for a show. Her classical training and innate talent helped her see into Gershwin's soul to play sympathetically. From this musical rapport grew a deep and abiding love; Kay became one of the few real loves of George Gershwin's life.

So as they worked on their next show, the clever brothers set up their own double entendre, writing a show titled, *Oh, Kay!* George rarely reflected on anything. He was too busy. Ira preferred a slower, more thoughtful pace. Ira actually kept journals recording both his and his brother's lives. In some cases, the lyrics he wrote for his brother's tunes kept pace with the feelings and events that colored his talented sibling's life. More often they were a parody of those feelings and events. *Oh Kay!* is more than just a pun on a popular expression. With his characteristic sardonic, lyrical wit, Ira is poking fun at brother George's love live once again.

In the second act Gertrude Lawrence, in her first starring role, was on stage to sing a tender ballad, "Someone to Watch Over Me." The song had its beginning as a rhythm tune, bouncing along at a swing tempo akin to the usual setting of "I've Got Rhythm." As such, it was a forgettable melody. Musing in the 1950s, brother Ira remarked, "As originally conceived by the composer, this tune would probably not be around today. At the piano in its early existence it was fast and jazzy, and undoubtedly I would have written it up as another dance-and-ensemble number. One day, for no particular reason and hardly aware of what he was at, George started and continued it in a comparatively slow tempo; and half of it hadn't sounded when both of us had the same reaction..."

Oh Kay! was a hit, and "Someone to Watch Over Me" became a standard overnight. That was some seventy-five years ago. That was just one song of the hundreds George and Ira Gershwin created.

The death of George Gershwin is one of the tragedies of American Song. Following the move to Hollywood Gershwin seemed preoccupied, temperamental, plagued with headaches and other complaints. Friends grew concerned, while Ira and his wife Leonora attributed his malaise to "Hollywooditis"—having too much time and too little to do. Medical tests failed to discover any problems after he experienced blackouts during performances and blinding headaches for days. In fact, George Gershwin was suffering the effects of a long growing brain tumor. The tumor was threatening his life by the time it was found. Surgery was immediate and unsuccessful. At only 38 years old the brilliant light of Gershwin's genius went out forever. We are left to wonder what he might have accomplished. We are left to sing and celebrate the great oeuvre he left behind. A very partial list includes the following standards and shows:

But Not for Me	'S Wonderful
Embraceable You	Someone to Watch Over Me
Fascinating Rhythm	Summertime
Let's Call the Whole Thing Off	They All Laughed
Oh, Lady Be Good	They Can't Take That Away from Me
Nice Work if You Can Get It	The Man I Love
A Foggy Day	Somebody Loves Me
But Not For Me	Embraceable You
I Got Rhythm	How Long Has This Been Going On?
Love Walked In	Our Love Is Here To Stay
An American in Paris	Rhapsody in Blue
Porgy and Bess	

Take the A Train

Billy Strayhorn

By 1938 Billy had his job in the drugstore, and his dreams. The slight young man who dreamed of "jazz and cocktails in the very gay places on the wheel of life, to get the feel of life," went to work every morning at the Pennfield Pharmacy, a corner store in a poor section of Pittsburgh. Patrons would call in for some ice cream; Billy would deliver it and entertain them with a song or two. Evenings he might entertain for a cocktail party or social event. The fun days of High School Theater were over, but Billy Strayhorn still wrote, studied, arranged and played his piano. Later a famous standard itself, his "Lush Life" was written in Pittsburgh while Billy was only eighteen years old. And he still lived at home, caught between a cynical, burnt out father, and the mother who shared Billy's heart and his dreams.

Then the break came. A friend from the drugstore, a pharmacy student named David Perelman, had a classmate whose uncle knew Duke Ellington. And the wheels of destiny began to turn. Billy got the chance to meet the famous Duke.

By 1938 Duke Ellington was in full swing—a brilliant pianist, composer, entertainer, the preeminent black bandleader of the world. When the Duke Ellington orchestra swung through Pittsburgh, Billy's friend's uncle came through. After a brief meeting backstage at Ellington's matinee performance, Strayhorn was invited to the Duke's dressing room at the massive Stanley Theater. Usually shy and insecure, nicknamed "Swee' Pea" because of his diminutive stature and thick glasses, the 24-year-old delivery boy came to life when Duke sat him down at the piano. Ellington reclined on the couch in his huge drawing room, his eyes closed, ready to be unimpressed.

"Let me hear what you can do."

Strayhorn stormed his future: "Now, this is how you play it." He played, flawlessly, through "Sophisticated Lady," an Ellington standard. He played it exactly as Duke had done it.

"I might do it like this." He then added syncopation, trills and flurries, and reinterpreted the same song with such panache, even the Duke himself looked over the piano player's shoulder with awe and admiration.

"Go get Harry," Duke ordered a nearby musician. "Can you do that again?" After, of course, a perfect rendition of the tune in Ellington's own style, Strayhorn began reharmonizing and improvising over the Duke's famous "Solitude," now with Ellington's hands on his shoulders. A small crowd of Ellington's arrangers and musicians assembled.

Duke Ellington was impressed. In fact, he immediately wanted Billy to work with him. Neither of them knew how it could be arranged, however. Duke had no need of a second piano player; after all, he was Duke Ellington, and he played the piano. He was an arranger and composer himself, and he had several other musicians in his orchestra working on arrangements. The band was in the middle of a long road trip, with no room and no time for extras. But he couldn't overlook the talent of this young Mozart. He couldn't let him get away. Something had to be worked out.

After writing an arrangement or two for the band during their Pittsburgh stay, Billy had to let the Duke Ellington Orchestra sweep out of town. Before they left, Ellington paid Strayhorn twenty dollars for an arrangement he liked, and sketched directions to his apartment in Harlem. "After the tour," Duke promised, "we'll get together." Swee' Pea wondered if this would be all that would come of his introduction to the Duke.

"Off they went," Strayhorn recalled. "And off I went—back home and back to the drugstore."

Billy waited for weeks, with no word from Ellington. But he felt something beyond hope; he knew it had to happen. He felt destined for New York, for "jazz and cocktails," for the life he dreamed. A friend loaned him the money for the train fare, and Billy prepared to leave home for the big city, guided by that carefully folded paper with directions to Duke's apartment. He read the quickly scrawled note so many times it became a kind of symbol. A map to his destiny. Again and again he unfolded the notepaper, over and over he read: "Take the A Train to Harlem."

He wanted something special to impress the great man once more. He intuitively knew he must not rely on the memory of an evening on the road in Pittsburgh to create an opportunity for his talent in Ellington's constellation. He had to do it again, he had to wow them all over again!

As he later told the story, the music and lyrics to "Take the A Train" came to him effortlessly and almost immediately. He worked the tune out in his mind. He read his little note with the directions that were now becoming a lyric. He ran errands, clerked the drug store, made deliveries, and all day long, "Take the A Train" swirled through his mind, growing, evolving, gathering energy, taking shape. By the time he sat down at the piano, the song had a life of its own. "It was like writing a letter to a friend," the composer reflected.

By January of 1939 Strayhorn once again caught up with Duke Ellington, now in Newark, New Jersey. "Duke, here's that young man." Someone from the entourage signaled The Duke. No one remembered his name. But Ellington was glad to see the prodigy, and hurried him to a piano. Billy played his "Take the A Train."

"Guess what?" Billy phoned home to Pittsburgh. "I'm going to work for Duke. I played that tune 'A Train' for him, and he liked it. I'm moving to New York!"

White Christmas

Irving Berlin

It is impossible to overestimate the importance of Irving Berlin to popular music. When Jerome Kern said, "He has no place in American music, he IS American music," he wasn't indulging in hyperbole. Berlin had an uncanny capacity to capture the spirit of the country and sum it up in song. In hit after hit he evoked the ethos of three generations!

Of course, the man who embodies the American Pop Tune was born in Siberia! On May 11, 1888, little Israel Baline came into the world in Temun, Russian Siberia. When Israel was only four years old, the family (seven brothers and sisters) fled a Czarist pogrom and landed, penniless, in New York's Lower East Side. By the time Israel turned eight, his father had died. Israel worked the streets as a newsboy to help support the family. Later he became a singing waiter, then a song plugger for Tony Pastor's Music Hall in Union Square. By twenty he taught himself to play piano, changed his name to Irving Berlin (an Americanized homonym), and started writing songs.

Irving scored his first big hit in 1911. He was twenty-three years old. The song was *Alexander's Ragtime Band.* It is over ninety years later, now, and you know the tune! Ragtime was already a fad, but with the publication of *Alexander's Ragtime Band,* it became an international sensation, and young Irving Berlin became—famous! He married, but lost his bride, Dorothy Goetz, to typhoid soon after their honeymoon. When the United States went to war in 1917, Berlin enlisted as a private. He produced all-soldier shows to boost morale, and his song, "Oh, How I Hate to Get Up in the Morning" became the anthem of the Army, as popular as George M. Cohan's "Over There." (You know them, too!)

After the Great War it was back to Broadway. Writing for Ziegfeld he cranked out show tunes, one after another. Royalties increased, so he started his own publishing company. When he fell in love with Ellin Mackay, the result was love songs like, "Always" and "All Alone." She would become the second Mrs. Irving Berlin. By then Mr. Berlin was no stranger to movies. In 1927, Al Jolson had sung one of Berlin's songs in *The Jazz Singer,* the first successful talking feature film. The song, "Blue Skies," written in 1926, would prove to be one of Berlin's most enduring standards. It has been recorded thousands of times—and you know it too, don't you? He wrote for Jolson again, a follow-up hit called "Mammy." Then, discouraged with the quality of sound in the talkies, he returned to New York. But the return was short-lived. With the Depression curtailing the New York theater scene, Berlin moved to Hollywood, where hard times just meant increased demand for cheap entertainment, escape, and musicals. By the time the Great Depression drove him back to California, the Hollywood musical was coming of age, and with it, the famous Irving Berlin.

Songs flowed freely out of Berlin's collaboration with Hollywood, songs that define the musical to this day, songs that we all hum, songs that you wish you heard more of...songs like "Top Hat, "White Tie and Tails," which will always belong to Fred Astaire. Or the immortal "Cheek to Cheek," also first sung by Astaire with Ginger Rogers in the musical *Top Hat.* Astaire tells the story in his autobiography, <u>Steps in Time</u>, that Rogers wore a feathered dress for the movie scene, and was, in fact, shedding profusely. "I had feathers in my ears, my mouth, all over the front of my suit..."

Top Hat, along with *42nd Street, Footlight Parade* and others, helped define the '30s musical as an identifiable genre, and Irving Berlin was its acknowledged master. For *Follow the Fleet* he wrote "Let's Face the Music and Dance." In 1938 Twentieth Century Fox produced a huge musical devoted entirely to the music of Irving Berlin, featuring such standards as "What'll I Do," "Easter Parade," and, of course, "Alexander's Ragtime Band"—the movie's title. When the nation once again went to war, Berlin tapped into the heartfelt spirit of America to create "God Bless America." It was sung first by Kate Smith over the radio waves, and then it was sung in homes and churches and synagogues, at bond rallies and USO shows, in railroad stations and mess halls around the world at war. Once more, Irving

Berlin, the Siberian songsmith, managed to put America's heart into words and music. He assigned all royalties, in perpetuity, to the Boy Scouts and Girl Scouts of America.

In 1942 he wrote a score for a Paramount picture, *Holiday Inn.* The story line featured Bing Crosby (then a gigantic star) as an entertainer who plans to live in the country and manage an inn, putting on thematic shows for various holidays. The device allowed Berlin to retread a comfortable favorite, "Easter Parade," and called for him to create several more songs around holiday material. For Valentine's Day he wrote a song destined to be a timeless standard, "Be Careful, It's My Heart." He summed up the plot's romantic rivalry between Astaire and Crosby over co-star Marjorie Reynolds with "You're Easy to Dance With." And for Christmas, he wrote a little number, introduced humbly with Crosby and Marjorie Reynolds (dubbed by Martha Mears) called *White Christmas.*

There is no dramatic story to the writing. There is little drama to Berlin's methodology. He simply sat at his piano and transcribed the soul of America. It is that simple, and that extraordinary. *White Christmas* became the best selling sheet music in history. For decades it held the record for single record sales as well. The second movie to include the song (and singer Bing Crosby), this one titled *White Christmas,* came out in 1954. It may have been meant to cash in on the popularity of the song, but it served to further establish it as the official ballad of Christmas. And that is only the beginning of the success of *White Christmas.* While other songs now may rival it in sales, nothing can come close in sentiment.

As individuals we each associate memories with songs. Many folks have a tune or two they think of as "our song." A song comes on the radio, and you are instantly transported to Ocean City, New Jersey, 1962, or to Red Rock, Colorado, in 1977, or Paris in the '40s...all of us have our images, our memories, our stories. Only one song seems to have the unique power to move virtually all of us to a sweet, nostalgic Spirit of Christmas. There is an elegant sadness to the lyric, a wistful longing for the way it "used to be," for the Christmas we wish we might have, but know we will never experience. Still for all that, tearful or merry, home or far away, once Bing Crosby sings *White Christmas,* then it's Christmas in America.

Irving Berlin continued to introduce many more hits to stage and screen, such as the memorable "There's No Business like Show Business," or the play *Annie Get Your Gun,* introduced in the '40s and revived as recently as the turn of the century. And he lived to enjoy his status as America's songwriter for over 100 years.

Seven Come Eleven

Charlie Christian

The brief life of Charlie Christian is the stuff of legend. He burst on the scene from nowhere, his candle burned brightly for two short years, then he was forever gone. The legacy he left would dramatically change jazz, and virtually reinvent the guitar.

Charlie Christian was born in Texas and grew up in the poorest ghetto of Oklahoma City. His father was a blind street musician. Charlie grew up leading his dad through the streets so he could play guitar and beg for spare change. Later, young Charlie made guitars from cigar boxes to accompany his father. With his brothers, the family made an impromptu band. At school Charlie fell under the influence of some good teachers, especially Mrs. Porkbonnet, who encouraged him to develop his musical talent and understanding.

As the rangy young guitarist grew, so did his genius. He was sitting in with local orchestras by his early teens. Those days, the 1930s, saw the first working amplification of the electric guitar. The New Orleans jazz bands that introduced the new music to America in the 1920s used banjos, drums and bass to drive the beat. The banjo was simply louder than any guitar, its treble attack pierced through the brass, while the early steel-stringed guitars reflected their Spanish classical ancestors, with deeper tones and small, thin-waisted bodies. When Orville Gibson hired Lloyd Loar to design a guitar with an arched top and "F holes," resembling a violin or cello in design, the guitar became an option for the orchestra. Big, loud arch-tops like the Gibson L-5, Strombergs and Epiphones featured prominently in the bands of the '20s and '30s. The round, rich tone of the guitar was more versatile and less strident than the banjo. Still the guitar remained almost exclusively in the rhythm section. All that was about to change.

When George Beauchamp and Adolph Rickenbacker developed a system for transmitting the sound of the guitar through an electrical amplification system, the purpose had still been to make it louder as a rhythm instrument. Pioneers of jazz guitar like Eddie Lang, Carl Kress and Lonnie Johnson had experimented with single string melody and obligato lines in small ensembles, and Django Rinehart was trading single note licks with violinist Stephane Grappelli in their Quintette of the Hot Club of Paris. But it all came together under the magical fingers of Charlie Christian.

Christian listened to the soloists of his era. He heard Louis Armstrong, Bix Beiderbecke, Fletcher Henderson, Benny Goodman and others. With the help of a crude amplifier, he approached his guitar as a solo instrument. The lines he invented are now classic. His solos were original, complex, challenging. He heard the music in such a unique way, he played outside the chords. He used diminished scales, flatted 9th and 11th note runs—in short, he played brilliantly. He played solos like a horn. In Oklahoma City, everyone talked about Charlie.

Then John Hammond came to town. Hammond is another of the great legendary figures of jazz. The ultimate impresario. Born wealthy (grandson to the Vanderbilt family), he devoted his life to discovering new musical talent, elevating the place of jazz in American music, and to breaking down the color barriers thrown up by racial prejudice that he saw in music and in American life. For over fifty years he promoted careers as diverse as Billie Holiday and Bruce Springsteen. He was passing through Oklahoma City, scouting the so-called territory bands, when he decided to check out Charlie Christian. He was blown away! No one played guitar like Charlie. This was a radical reinterpretation of a musical instrument. This was musical history. He had to see Charlie go all the way. Hammond, with his formidable influence and will, set out to make it happen.

He called his brother-in-law, Benny Goodman. The "King of Swing" had to hear this amazing new guitarist. Benny was on the West Coast then, reviving his band in another tour through California. He didn't care much about guitars, they were only rhythm instruments, and he had a perfectly good guitarist now. Hammond insisted, "You've got to hear this kid play."

The kid from Oklahoma arrived in L.A., "carrying his guitar in a gunny sack." Pictures of the historic meeting reveal a 19-year-old Charlie Christian, a young black man wearing an ill-fitting green suit, looking lost and bewildered, surrounded by natty, intense, white musicians and businessmen. He didn't fit in.

Hammond had absolutely forced Goodman to listen to Charlie Christian. Goodman himself was a force to be reckoned with, and he didn't like taking orders. With a small ensemble he told the Okie with the guitar to play the rhythm for a song or two. They played through the numbers and Goodman left, unimpressed. Christian's rhythm playing was nothing too great, Benny reported to Hammond. The two left for the club where Goodman's band was performing.

This is where the legend gets going. John Hammond had heard Charlie Christian play, and immediately recognized world-changing genius. He knew Goodman had not really heard Charlie do what he was capable of doing. Goodman said play rhythm, so the easy-going, shy 19-year-old played chords, like the guitarists of that time. He did a passable job. But that was not Charlie's genius. The evening got underway. After Goodman's first set the orchestra took a break, and Hammond went to work. When Benny took the stage for the second set he noticed the tall, lanky teenager on stage with his orchestra, guitar in hand. He glared at Hammond with an angry withering stare, then called the tune, "Rose Room." He was reasonably sure the new kid wouldn't know the song, and if he did, they would lay down a few verses, then dismiss him. The band played through the head, or melody, and Benny blew a solo verse. Then something happened. Something that had never happened before.

Christian jammed over the song with licks that any clarinetist would envy. He invented intricacies that Goodman himself would use from that day on—and Goodman knew it. Dumbfounded, he took another verse, then handed it back to the strange, new guitarist. Charlie did it again, only better. With every verse, Christian found new lines. They traded licks—this kid could play anything on his guitar that Benny could make up with his clarinet. And when they reversed roles, with Goodman trying to echo Charlie's lines, well, the "King of Swing" had some woodshedding to do. History was being made, as the Benny Goodman orchestra played "Rose Room" for forty-five minutes! When the song was over, Christian had a job with the world famous Benny Goodman orchestra. The Benny Goodman quintet became a sextet on the spot!

Who knows what might have happened had Charlie Christian lived to fulfill his destiny. As it was, he toured with the band for the duration of the West Coast swing. He returned with them to New York and played guitar for Goodman for roughly a year and a half. During his year and a half in Harlem, Christian sat in with Dizzy Gillespie, Theolonius Monk and Charlie Parker at the legendary Minton's Playhouse jam sessions, helping to invent the vocabulary of be-bop. It was just an after-hours jam session, at a small club on 118th Street, but it attracted the best players in jazz, and they laid the foundations for most modern jazz, there at Minton's, night after night. Some claim that Charlie actually invented the term be-bop, but who can say today? He toured with the orchestra, played the uptown gigs, jammed with the geniuses at Minton's and recorded a few sides with Goodman's orchestra and sextet. He lived, when not on the road, in a hotel room in Harlem. Little is known of his private life, either before his sudden stardom or after. He was described as quiet, even shy. He always seemed happy. He was remarkably easy going, nothing seemed to bother him. In fact, he was probably stoned most of the time. Marijuana was in common use in the jazz circles of the time, and Charlie was known to have a fondness for the weed that went beyond the occasional weekend high.

By the winter of 1941, Charlie Christian was 22, famous, and sick. If he had not lived such an intense life, so lost in his music, he may have been able to beat back the TB. But it was not an easy disease to beat in 1941. The cigarettes and marijuana that had weakened his lungs continued to hurt him as he continued to use them. Even in the Staten Island sanitarium where Goodman's personal physician sent Charlie in hopes of recovery, Christian loved to sneak out with friends for a party, or catch a reefer in a restroom. And so, the seminal genius of lead guitar was lost to the world at age 22.

Everyone was influenced by Charlie Christian. Barney Kessel got to meet him, and Christian became his hero. From Wes Montgomery, Kenny Burrell, Les Paul, to Howard Alden or Joe Pass, no one plays single line lead guitar without a debt to Charlie Christian, whether conscious or unknown. His enormous influence is all out of proportion to his recorded output. We have the sides he recorded with the sextet, such cuts as "A Sm-oooth One" and "Flying Home." A few of the Minton's jam sessions were recorded by Jerry Newman, an amateur with a tape machine. And we have a song or two actually credited to Christian's composition. Of those, "Seven Come Eleven" has made its way into the repertoire as a standard because of its clever head (melody) and easy jam. It is a tune with no words, designed to be jammed around, offering a starting point for improvisation. A happy song, it is usually played without the tragic ghost of Charlie Christian hanging around. Yet year after year guitar players title albums "For Charlie."

Anyone learning jazz guitar simply has to study his fretwork. Herb Ellis, one of the great jazz guitarists of all time, assesses Christian's skill: "If Charlie was alive today, we would still all be learning from him. He was just that good."

He burst on the scene from nowhere, his candle burned brightly for two years, then he was forever gone. But we have "Seven Come Eleven."

I've Told Every Little Star

Jerome Kern

In 1902 Jerry Kern entered the family business in Newark, New Jersey. He wanted to be a musician. His father insisted, despite the plaudits Jerry had gathered at the high school play, that he could do that at night. By day he would be a merchant. Shortly after he began his employment he was sent into the Bronx to purchase a few pianos. It was his father's gesture of concession—the store could stock one or two pianos for Jerry to sell, and play. The next day the horse drawn vans began to arrive at Woolf & Co. Later, Jerry loved to regale, "You can't imagine what it looks like for two hundred pianos to come off vans." Henry Kern said to his son, "I think I'm going into the piano business. As for you, I think you should become a musician." And that is how it all began.

By 1914 Jerome Kern had teamed up with Lyricist P. G. Wodehouse—yes, the P. G. Wodehouse who gave us Psmith (the "P" is silent, as in "pshrimp"), Bertie Wooster and his beloved butler, Jeeves. The P. G. Wodehouse who wrote most of *Vanity Fair* for many years under a flurry of pseudonyms (the "p" is silent). Guy Bolton added a third to their partnership, writing the book for their musical efforts. Those efforts centered on the Princess Theatre, off Broadway at 104 West Thirty-ninth St. The team worked with Bessie Marbury and Ray Comstock to create seamless shows, where the music actually served to advance the plot. These shows went beyond the thoughtless reviews then popular, they were the forerunners of today's musical theatre. Kern's musical genius drove these productions, and earned him a reputation as a young man with an auspicious future.

That future might never have happened but for a twist of fate and a card game. On May 1, 1915, Jerome Kern had plans to sail to

England. The well known producer Charles Frohman was sailing on *Lusitania,* and Jerry looked forward to working with him. But Jerry loved card games. It was an addiction he never really got over. That last night of April, 1915, Jerry was up all night in a hot poker game. This was one gamble he won—big. Jerry woke up at 11:30 in the morning. He rushed to the dock, only to watch as his ship steamed out of the harbor. He had "missed the boat." Six days later *Lusitania* was torpedoed off the coast of Ireland by a German U-boat. Her sinking is one of the greatest maritime tragedies, losing 1,195 lives. The impact of such a narrow escape motivated the young composer as nothing else could do.

Jerome Kern was on a mission. He wanted to reinvent American Musical Theater. In Oscar Hammerstein II he found a perfect co-inventor. When the team brought *Showboat* to the stage at the National Theatre in Washington, D.C., on November 15, 1927, history was made. Critic Miles Krueger summed it up: "The history of American Musical Theatre, quite simply, is divided in two eras: everything before *Showboat* and everything after *Showboat.*" *Showboat* did what Kern had dreamed of doing. It created an integrated book, the music drove the plot forward, the songs captured and enhanced the drama of the scenes. Oscar Hammerstein had a fantastic gift of penning a winsome lyric for seemingly any occasion or narrative contrivance. And Kern's melodies made them work. Because of *Showboat,* offers biographer Lee Davis, "Jerry was and will always remain the true father of the American musical."

What do you do when you are the father of the American musical at 42? Jerry had his passions. He could not resist cards, he collected rare books, antique furniture and stamps. He was growing wealthy, as royalties rolled in from his popular compositions. He and his wife, Eva, had one daughter, Betty. He loved to argue, in public—just for the fun of it. And he enjoyed a good "practical joke." He once made a bet he could single-handedly shut down a construction project in London. Well and expensively attired, he began to inspect the site. He appeared to be pleased, and after a thorough inspection, he complimented the foreman on a job well done. Then he suggested the entire crew take the rest of the day off, with pay. He won the bet. Another time when a neighbor refused, for some reason, to cut his grass, Jerry simply had a herd of sheep released on the lawn. His friends included Irving Berlin and Cole Porter, while his understudies included Richard Rodgers (informally) and George Gershwin (formally).

Then, there are the songs. Throughout his life, Jerome Kern consistently wrote among the most brilliant and beautiful melodies in song. His output was phenomenal. Consider this very partial list:

All the Things You Are	The Way You Look Tonight
The Song Is You	Smoke Gets in Your Eyes
Long Ago (And Far Away)	Yesterdays
I'm Old Fashioned	Pick Yourself Up
A Fine Romance	Let's Begin
I Won't Dance	They Didn't Believe Me
She Didn't Say Yes	The Last Time I Saw Paris
Ol' Man River	Can't Help Loving That Man of Mine

Concerning "They Didn't Believe Me," Alec Wilder writes in his benchmark *American Popular Song: The Great Innovators, 1900–1950:* " I cannot conceive how the alterations of a single note could do other than harm the song." Cabaret star Mary Cleere Haran calls "The Way You Look Tonight" the most beautiful song ever written. She might be right. While countless musicians and composers think of Kern's "All the Things You Are" as, in the words of Lee Davis, "the one perfect popular song," or "the greatest song ever written."

It seems remarkable then, that these immortal songs were not written under the spell of any particular inspiration. They were simply what the plot called for. When *Swing Time* needed a sarcastic love song, Kern came up with "A Fine Romance." If a sad ballad about life on the river was called for, "Ol' Man River" flowed forth. "Lovely to Look At" was born when the movie version of *Roberta* needed a tune to double as a romance and modeling scene. (See Dorothy Fields and "The Way You Look Tonight.") "The Last Time I Saw Paris" was written, in 1941, for a city which had just been occupied by Nazi Germany.

The one unusual inspiration Kern cites was a sea bird. He heard a bird trilling outside his window once, on vacation at his cousin's Nantucket home. The melody found a way into his mind, and when it came back out, it was as, "I've Told Every Little Star."

He wrote every day, on his beloved Bluthner piano. In 1937 the family moved permanently to Hollywood, after a decade of coastal commuting for Jerome. When they moved into their Beverly Hills home, Jerry discovered that the movers had drilled a bolt right into the sound board of his piano. He bellowed in pain. Six days later he had his heart attack. While recuperating in Cedars of Lebanon hospital, Jerry sustained another blow when his friend and pupil, George Gershwin, died in that same hospital, a few floors below Jerry, at age 38.

Jerry was 64 years old in November, 1945, when he met with his old friend and first collaborator, Guy Bolton, in Manhattan. They talked over old times, sharing lunch at the Lambs Club. They made tentative plans to work on a show together in the near future. After lunch Jerry walked to the corner of Park Avenue and 57th St. where he collapsed with a cerebral hemorrhage. He lingered in Doctor's Hospital for six days, before dying with his family and friends present. Oscar Hammerstein was softly singing one of Jerry's favorite creations, "I've Told Every Little Star," the Nantucket bird song, as Jerome Kern breathed his last. Hammerstein said, in his eulogy of his friend, that Kern "...devoted all his lifetime to giving the world something it needs and knows it needs—beauty."

Giant Steps

John Coltrane

How did Coltrane do it? He just kept getting better. Born in North Carolina in 1926, he learned to love and play music from his multi-instrumentalist father. He first played alto horn and clarinet, then switched to tenor by high school. He studied at the Ornstein School of Music in Philadelphia, then did a hitch in a Navy band from 1946-47. By then, he was a pro.

After the Navy he joined a band led by Joe Webb. From there he would go on to play as a sideman with the most progressive, luminous leaders in jazz, including Dizzy Gillespie, Johnny Hodges, Theolonius Monk and Miles Davis.

His playing featured prominently on Miles' landmark, *Kind of Blue.* Jazz critic Zita Carno described Coltrane's tone: "An incredibly powerful, resonant and sharply penetrating sound with a spine-chilling quality." In the history of jazz he may be best known for the fierce solos he blew on *Kind of Blue,* especially when contrasted to Cannonball Adderley's alto. His style became known as "sheets of sound."

> I know some people think Coltrane was playing anger through his horn, but his music was very intense. Coltrane's music is about love to me, and love can be very intense...to a person who is not in tune, it can appear to be very negative, and very angry..."
> —Jack DeJohnett, *Down Beat,* Nov. 2, 1978

Art Davis called his music "volcanic." Nat Hentoff adds, "One quality that can always be expected from Coltrane is intensity. He asks so much of himself..."

In 1957 Coltrane went through what he described as a spiritual awakening. This awakening was reflected in his subsequent music, most notably in 1964's *A Love Supreme*. You can hear this three part composition of sacred music performed every Sunday, at San Francisco's St. John Coltrane's African Orthodox Church. But be warned, this is not sacred music as you might usually define the term. This is straight ahead jazz, dedicated to God, seeking for something, grasping for the divine, with all the emotional intensity that scared the critics.

1960 was a pivotal year for Coltrane. He formed his quartet, and recorded his album, *Giant Steps*. The title song categorically answered our question, "How did Coltrane do it?" The answer: Chops. Coltrane could blow. Quite apart from questions of tone—soft and breathy versus clear and dynamic; apart from debates about anger and love, apart from all the speculations about what the music means, John Coltrane flew through the baffling changes of *Giant Steps* in a way that left listeners breathless, and horn players feeling like they were leaving a magic show: "How'd he do that?"

Coltrane said the song was named for the bass line: "…the bass line is kind of a loping one. It goes from minor thirds to fourths, kind of a lop-sided pattern in contrast to moving strictly in fourths or in half-steps."

Then there is Richard Rodgers, the prolific composer encountered in several chapters of this book. Back in 1937 he worked with a stellar team including partner Larry Hart, writers Moss Hart and George S. Kaufman (with whom he argued fiercely), George M. Cohan and producer Sam Harris to create a Broadway play, *I'd Rather Be Right*. The show, a political satire mocking Roosevelt, went over rather well; it was a mild hit. The score was generally regarded as mediocre, but one song from *I'd Rather Be Right* took on a life of its own.

"Have You Met Miss Jones?" originally sung by Cohan, describing his secretary, instantly won the respect of the jazz community. The song starts out as nothing unusual. The verse goes through a comforting chord pattern where everything follows as expected. Then the bridge hits. Two bars each for A flat, G flat, D major, back to G flat, and round to F—the original key. In other words, the bridge flies through key changes at a bewildering pace. Rodgers uses enharmonic theory, devising a melody that somehow holds the whole thing together and makes it sing. And sing it does—the tune is bouncy and adorable! It caught on instantly.

Now listen again to *Giant Steps*. Those inexplicable changes, the wall of sound that outlines chord after chord in seemingly random connections—it all sounds familiar. Sing:

> Then all at once I lost my breath,
> And all at once I was scared to death

over the complex and chaotic polyphony and you are on to the secret of "Giant Steps." In the days of be-bop it was quite common to devise new "heads" to popular tunes. Everyone jammed Gershwin's "I've Got Rhythm," using their own melodies and counter melodies, so much that the song came to be known simply as "Rhythm Changes." And old "Have You Met Miss Jones?" found a new life when its bridge was reincarnated as the basic foundation for Coltrane's intimidating standard, "Giant Steps."

Today "Giant Steps" is in the repertoire. Any aspiring player needs to know it, and jam it. And "Have You Met Miss Jones?" continues to be performed as a standard in its own right. Quite a gal, that Miss Jones!

Ornithology

Charlie Parker, Benny Harris,
Morgan Lewis and Nancy Hamilton

It began with a nice, gentle love song. "How High the Moon" was written by Morgan Lewis Jr. as a medium swing ballad, for the 1940 revue *Two for the Money*. Lyrics were added by Nancy Hamilton, to create a song of longing for love: "Until you will, how still my heart, How High the Moon."

This was a time of great experimentation in popular song writing. For these golden hours, the popular songs were jazz. Writers like Jerome Kern, the Gershwins, Richard Rodgers, Cole Porter, and many others consistently pushed concepts of time and tonality. The II/V/I turn-around chord progression had replaced the old I/IV/V, allowing a far greater span on improvisation. Now one song, in 32 bars, could move through half a dozen traditional key signatures. While that is difficult to play, once grasped it means that any good instrumentalist has a limitless number of scales to work with. It is probably this characteristic that best defines and sets apart the jazz song.

The melody to "How High the Moon" had the good fortune of moving through these changes with irresistible charm. Beginning in G major, Hamilton's tune goes through F major, E flat major, G minor, back to G major, up to A, down to G, and then repeats! And it all sounds—inevitable. For the serious jazz virtuoso, "How High the Moon" presented a chance to shine!

Meanwhile, back at Minton's after hours jam session, Dizzy Gillespie, Charlie Christian and Charlie Parker were pushing the envelope of tonality so far out of shape it no longer looked like an envelope. They had to call it something else. Someone labeled their music "be-bop," and the label stuck. Be-bop wove diminished and flat five scales around all the chords in the song. It called for awesome technique, and used virtually every note of the chromatic palate. A couple of be-bop jammers could play through the changes to "How High the Moon" for an hour, and never repeat a lick. So, they did.

Eventually, after countless hours of running through the chord progression, Charlie Parker settled into a new, vastly more complex melody line to fit over the chords of "How High the Moon." It was intended, as with all be-bop heads, as a starting place. A line to work from—a "head." The brilliant, mercurial Alto Sax phenomenon had a nickname, of course. For various reasons. (Who knows the real story, if there is one?) Charlie Parker was known first as Yardbird, then just as Bird. So when his head to "How High the Moon" caught on, it, too, received a nickname. The Bird's head was named, in his honor: "Ornithology."

Kind of Blue, So What

Miles Davis

It wasn't just *"So What."* It was the entire album—the famous sessions now known as *Kind of Blue.* *"So What"* is the most popular song to come from the album that changed jazz forever. With *Kind of Blue* Miles Davis became a superstar, and Jazz became an uncharted, promising, experimental territory once more, for a new generation of explorers.

Always aloof and "cool," Miles Davis simply sketched a few modal scales for most of the album, passed them around, and rolled tape. The tunes were recorded in a single take, after a few false starts. At least, that is the legend. Reality, of course, complicates things. Pianist Bill Evans actually co-wrote several of the songs, and had been working on them for months prior to that fateful afternoon at Columbia's 30th St. Studio. Davis never credited him, beyond sending one royalty check for $25.00.

Much of the genius of *Kind of Blue* comes, simply, from the collection of talent—the sum is at least the whole of its parts. And Miles Davis assembled the finest talent around. Bill Evans had left Davis' sextet after only seven months of playing and touring, complaining of "Crow Jim"—a reverse prejudice against Evans as the only white man in the band—or the audience. But he was back for the recording, with his understated rhythms, modal melodies, and classical voicings. For horns they had Miles on trumpet, with John Coltrane on tenor and Cannonball Adderley on alto. Paul Chambers, bass and James Cobb, drums, rounded out the rhythm section. Each soloist would go on to become a legend in his own right. This was a "Super Band."

They really were unfamiliar with the songs, and the entire style. Be-bop (by then the dominant jazz style) was filling complex chords with as many notes as possible. A soloist, to use a visual metaphor which many musicians employ, played down a stem, using any note that might fit the extended chord of the moment. Two beats to a chord, then on to the next stack. Any melody derived was just that, a derivation from the chords. This is a "vertical" approach, playing up and down a chord—stacked notes on a staff. Modes, on the other hand, are scales. They were part of any classical musician's training, but not much in use among jazz players until George Russell began his complex work on the "Lydian Chromatic Concept of Tonal Organization." Miles and his stellar team found in the modal concept a new approach to jazz. It has often been called a "return to melody." It was, essentially, horizontal. Musicians were not given a chord chart to play over, they were instead handed a set of scales to play through. Bill Evans' original liner notes explain *"So What:"*

> *"So What" is a simple figure based on 16 measures of one scale, and 8 of another and 8 more of the first, following a piano and bass introduction in a free rhythmic style."*

Later, Davis said his inspiration for *"So What"* came from two sources. One was African: with his girl friend (later wife) Frances Taylor he....

> *Went to this performance by the Ballet Africaine...Their rhythm! ...They would do rhythms like 5/4 and 6/8 and 4/4, and the rhythm would be changing and popping... When I first heard them play the finger piano that night and sing this song with the other guy dancing, man, that was some powerful stuff.*

His other influence was more nostalgic.

> *I added some other kind of sound I remembered from being back in Arkansas, when we were walking home from church and they were playing these bad gospels.*

That feeling was what I was trying to get close to...six years old, walking with my cousin along that Arkansas road.

Shortly after the album was released, Miles and a somewhat reconstituted sextet were featured on a rare national television broadcast, playing *"So What."* It became a popular hit. But critical response to the album was ambivalent. Some critics liked it, others did not. Many players were confused, it seemed so...simplistic. So open. So uncluttered. Where were the virtuoso flights through dazzling strings of 64th notes that had come to define jazz?

But the influence of the album spread, like the proverbial stone thrown into still waters. The still music of Modal Miles was rippling through the turbulent waters of be-bop. Musicians from Pee Wee Ellis (a founder of Funk) to Duane Allman, Andy Summers (of the Police) to Ray Manzarek (The Doors), Anthony Kiedis (Red Hot Chile Peppers) to Donald Fagen (Steely Dan), Gary Burton to Quincy Jones site *Kind of Blue* as a seminal influence. Miles himself moved on to quite different sounds and styles. But the brilliant work done in 1959 lingered, and took on a life of its own.

"So What" has been recorded at least 150 times, including noteworthy versions by Dexter Gordon, Frank Morgan, Benny Golson, John Stubblefield, Donald Harrison, Ronny Jordan, Jerry Garcia, Derek Trucks, Grant Green and George Benson.

Recorded over 40 years ago, *Kind of Blue* today sells roughly 7000 copies each week. The album did not reach gold certification (500,000 copies sold) until 1993. But by February of 1997 it went platinum (one million sold), and should reach triple platinum soon. As of this writing, *Kind of Blue* has its own web site at www.sonymusic.com/thelab/ConnecteD/MilesDavis, featuring an interactive analysis of *"So What"*.

Miles Davis died in 1991, after years of failing health. But his music shows up in the strangest places: In movies like *Pleasantville, In the Line of Fire,* or *Runaway Bride;* on eBay where several different versions of the album can be found for sale as collectibles.

Pianist Chick Corea comments,

> *It's one thing to just play a tune, or play a program of music, but it's another thing to practically create a new language of music, which is what Kind of Blue did.*

When contemporary trumpeters like Wallace Roney complain that, "Every time any trumpet player plays a mute, or lets in a little space, or sketches a gentle modal motif, he is compared to Miles Davis." Now that is high praise!

Curiosities

"I Never Knew That!"

"Many are interested in the how, why, even where, of the creation of classic songs. They are fascinated by their elusive, often unknown and unrecognized creators."

Too Marvelous for Words

Richard Whiting and
Johnny Mercer

Richard Whiting could never quite believe that he was really a song writer—until he met Johnny Mercer. Even though he went to work at Remick Publishing straight out of military school, on the strength of three of his songs; even though by 1914 he was making $30,000 in royalties. He threw away his biggest hit—literally threw it away!

With the outbreak of WW I the Michigan Theater in Detroit sponsored a war-song contest. Whiting sketched a lilting waltz, Ray Egan wrote a patriotic heart throb lyric called "Till We Meet Again." Whiting was convinced that the song was too boring, the tune too understated and the lyric to sappy to win any contest, so at the end of the day he crumpled the song sheet and tossed it in the trash basket. When his secretary at the office cleaned up, she found the crumpled sheet music, and decided to ask Mr. Jerome Remick (the owner) about it. His reply: "Let's not tell Richard." The team surreptitiously submitted the song, which went on to not only win the contest, but to become a favorite of the era, selling over five million copies of sheet music.

The Whiting family moved from Detroit to New York in 1928, where Richard's songs were regularly featured in Broadway revues, such as *George White's Scandals* and *Toot-Sweet*. By the following year they were among the first Broadway song writers to head for Hollywood. Warner Brothers first teamed Whiting with lyricist Johnny Mercer in 1937. Whiting was still the self-effacing, modest composer, "A dear fellow, too...modest and sweet, and not at all pushy like a lot of New York writers," observed Southern-born Mercer. Johnny Mercer, while charming, never seemed to lack for confidence.

Charged with three Warner musicals in one year, the team came through in spades. The movies are forgettable: *Ready, Willing and Able, Varsity Show,* and *Hollywood Hotel.* But the songs that came out of these movies went to reign on *Your Hit Parade,* and to endure as standards to today.

"Hurray for Hollywood" just opened the choir concert at my son's high school. Mercer and Whiting wrote it for *Hollywood Hotel,* seventy-four years ago. *Ready, Willing and Able* introduced "Too Marvelous for Words." Whiting's other titles include "The Lullaby of Broadway," "The Good Ship Lollipop," "She's Funny That Way," and "Beyond the Blue Horizon." "Too Marvelous for Words" has been covered by all the popular jazz singers, from Ella to Frank. It shows up regularly in movies. Any collection of Mercer hits, of which there are many, features "Too Marvelous for Words."

Mercer and Whiting formed a song writing team with tremendous potential, and everyone knew it. Even Dick Whiting was finally convinced that his was a wonderful talent. Then in the beginning of 1938, Richard Whiting suffered a completely unexpected heart attack. He simply collapsed and died on February 10, 1938. He was forty-six years old. Mercer would go on to numerous productive collaborations, with a wide spectrum of composers. But we will never know what they may have accomplished, had Mercer and Whiting been able to work together again.

Mr. Ed Meets Mona Lisa
Livingston and Evans

Everyone has heard of Jay Livingston and Ray Evans. You know them—you'll see. The boys met at the University of Pennsylvania where they formed an orchestra. They were so good they played cruise ships during vacations. On a stop in Havana they got into Latin rhythms, which so impressed the cruise director he promised them a job on any cruise ship in the Holland-America line. He could keep that promise because he was the head cruise director for the line. On subsequent sailings, they picked up Calypso timing in Trinidad, the Samba in Rio, and Argentine Tango in Buenos Aires.

Ray graduated at the top of his class from the famed Wharton School of Business, so he worked as an accountant in New York while the team struggled to break into Depression Era show biz as song writers. By 1941 the economy was looking up, and so was the future for Livingston and Evans. They wrote a few songs for the Broadway show, *Hellzapoppin,* including a Hit Parade money-maker, "G'Bye Now." In 1944 they made the move to Hollywood, where they teamed up with Johnny Mercer. Mercer was a legendary figure: songwriter, lyricist, singer and entertainer, founding president of Capitol Records, and at that time he was head of Paramount Pictures Music Department. The team wrote songs for Mercer's radio show. He got them in with producer Buddy DeSylva, who bit on "A Square in the Social Circle." By 1945 their tune "The Cat and the Canary" was up for an Academy Award. Ring any bells? Well, keep reading...

That same year they wrote "To Each His Own," for the picture of the same title. For three weeks in 1945, five of the Billboard Magazine Top Ten were covers of "To Each His Own." How about "Buttons and Bows?" Remember that? The boys wrote a song about Indians and the

Wild West for the Bob Hope, Jane Russell vehicle, *The Paleface.* They called it "Skookum." Director Norman McLeod hated it. Through some intense arguments McLeod held fast—he refused to work with the song. Dejected, Livingston and Evans dragged their tails back to the studio, to write "Buttons and Bows." It won the Oscar for 1948. Now they were the "Title Song Kings" in Hollywood. Studios lined up for movie themes. The '50s opened the golden age of television, and our team was there to set it to music.

Who can forget: *"A horse is a horse, of course, of course..."* They wrote themes for *Mr. Ed* and *Bonanza!* They wrote the haunting title song for *Tammy.* Another Bob Hope movie gave them their most timeless tune. Hope was starring in a Christmas movie, set in New York, *The Lemon Drop Kid.* Paramount wanted a new holiday song. The boys were skeptical: "Everyone sings the same old songs at Christmas." Still, if Irving Berlin could do it... They went to work. As the song evolved, it began to evoke the image of a Salvation Army Santa Claus ringing a little bell by his bucket. They called it "Tinkle Bells."

"Are you out of your mind? Do you know what the word 'tinkle' means?" This helpful comment came from Jay's wife, Lynn. They had to agree. But the tune was lovely, and it was so carefully thought through. They had actually written "Tinkle Bells" with verse and chorus over the same chords, so that they could be sung as a round, or in harmony, then added a lyric counterpoint to the chorus. They loved the singable, 3/4 time melody. They had to keep it. "What if we call it 'Silver Bells'?" Bing Crosby, AKA Mr. Christmas, was the first to record it (when Steve Lawrence and Edie Gorme were just kids), and it is now a beloved Christmas standard, with over 160 million records sold.

Alfred Hitchcock was making *The Man Who Knew Too Much* in 1955. He wanted Jimmy Stewart for the lead. Stewart's agent struck a deal. The director could get his star if he agreed to feature another client, Doris Day, in his movie, and (some agent!) if he signed another client, Livingston and Evans, to write a song for her to sing in the movie! Hitchcock told the team he wanted some foreign words in the title, and that Doris would be singing to her little boy in the scene. Doris Day hated the song they wrote: "Que Sera, Sera." She refused to sing it. Paramount Pictures insisted. She recorded it in one take, and afterwards said, "That's the last time you'll ever hear that song." Of course, it became one of Miss Day's biggest hits, and may be her signature song. It won Livingston and Evans their third Oscar.

Their greatest contribution to the jazz repertoire came in an equally unlikely manner. Paramount was making another WW II movie in 1949. This one was called *O.S.S.* starring Alan Ladd. The song they were asked to write was supposed to sound like an Italian folk song. In the movie it was to be sung as a warning— when the old radio went into their song, Alan Ladd could say "The Germans are coming." A secret code! They worked on a lush Romanesque melody, tentatively titled "Mona Lisa." Next, Paramount called in their song writers to tell them the new title for the film, *After Midnight.* Wouldn't that make a fine song? Keep the tune, just change the words. By now they were used to this. They barely complained. But when the 44-piece Paramount Orchestra assembled to record the demo for "After Midnight," they asked the singer to stick around, and record their "Mona Lisa" lyric as well, "Just for us." Then they read in Variety that the film had been retitled *Captain Carey, U. S.A.,* and "Mona Lisa" was back in... To no great acclaim. Sinatra tuned it down, Perry Como wouldn't touch it, even Vic Damone said no. The song's publisher, Larry Shayne, went after Nat King Cole. Cole was just transitioning from a hot, piano-playing jazz man who sings a little into the smooth, smoky-voiced balladeer. He said he recorded the song to get Shayne "out of my hair." They never expected it to become a hit. It won the Oscar for Livingston and Evans, their second, in 1950, and helped establish the romance of Nat King Cole's charm.

"Silver Bells," "Mona Lisa," "Mr. Ed," "Bonanza!" and "Que Sera, Sera." You know Livingston and Evans!

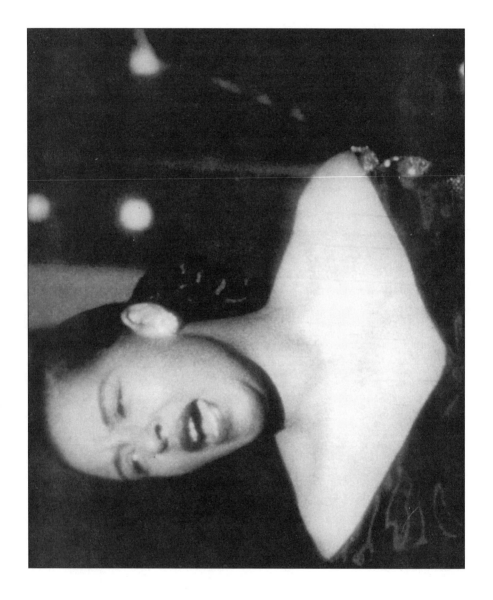

Strange Fruit

Abel Meeropol and Billie Holiday

Strange Fruit is a horrible song! One wealthy white patroness accosted Billie Holiday in the *Cafe Society* after an early rendition and instructed her, "Don't you dare ever sing that awful song again!" Billie closed nearly every show with it for the rest of her life.

The song is identified with Billie Holiday; it became one of her theme songs. It is identified with the civil rights struggle, it is a cry of protest, from the tortured black soul of America. Yet it was not written by Holiday, it was not written by a black songwriter at all.

Abel Meeropol was the author's name. For protection he wrote under the nom de plume, Lewis Allan. He was a Jewish high school teacher, and a full-boiled political activist. He was a member of the American Communist Party. When he saw a picture of the lynching, in 1937, of Thomas Shipp and Abram Smith, he was stirred to write a poem of protest. *Strange Fruit* was first published as a poem in the *New York Teacher;* later Meeropol submitted it to the Marxist journal, *New Masses*. In 1953, when Ethel and Julius Rosenberg were executed for treason, it would be the Meeropols who would adopt their children. He was also a big fan of Billie Holiday. When the diminutive teacher brought his poem, with a roughed out matching tune, to the *Café Society,* the barroom-brawling, hard-drinking, hard-cursing, twenty-four-year old Lady Day was scared to touch it. But by the show that evening, her mind was made up. After the first set she turned to band leader Frankie Newton and told him, *"Some guy brought me a hell of a damn song that I'm gonna do."*

Her friend and associate Danny Mendelsohn rewrote the melody, bringing it into Billie's style and range. The first time she sang the song, with only Danny and Art Herzog present, she didn't seem to understand the song, at first. Suddenly, Herzog recalls, *"...the impact of it hit her, and she put herself into the song."*

"Put" is far too mild a verb, Mr. Herzog. Billie lost herself into it, she abandoned her soul to the song. She immersed herself in it, and it in her. It became the cry of her soul, the cry of Black America. It was plaintive and defiant, daring and factual. In her imaginative autobiography, she said she wrote it; it had become, *"her song."*

It was a shocking song. Imagine closing a cabaret night, an evening of love songs. The standards of Jazz are filled with simple images: autumn leaves, a kiss, a nightingale sang, a foggy day, a stinger or two, and love, love, love. Drop into this mild, pleasing brew the explosive catalyst of a violent lynching, and the effect is devastating. The audience has been involved in an exchange with the artist, they have given their trust, inviting her to take them to new places. When the "place" is the deep south and the scene is *"The bulging eyes and twisted mouth,"*—expect a reaction. *"It is as if a game of let's pretend had ended and a blues singer who had been hiding her true sorrow in a set of love ditties had lifted the curtain and told us what it was that made her cry."* —Samuel Grafton, of the New York Post, described it, after a night at the *Café Society.*

Actress Billie Allen Henderson remembers hearing Billie Holiday sing *Strange Fruit* in 1952. *"I was trying to be sophisticated, and all of a sudden something stabs me in the solar plexus and I was gasping for air. It was so deeply felt...I could smell the burning flesh; I felt it...Nobody stirred...I thought, 'That's what art can do.'"*

People are still talking about it. *New York Times* and *Vanity Fair* contributor David Margolick recently wrote an entire book about *Strange Fruit,* the song that *Time Magazine* named, *"Song of the Century."* Writes Margolick:

> *Strange Fruit defies easy musical categorization and has slipped between the cracks of academic study. It's too artsy to be folk music, too explicitly political and polemical to be jazz. Surely no song in American history has ever been guaranteed to silence an audience or to generate such discomfort.*

In the *Boston Herald,* Larry Katz recently wrote:

> *"Holiday's rendition of* Strange Fruit *is the rare kind of performance that sears a listener's soul and leaves a permanent mark. The song is mournful, but Holiday sings it so gently, almost sweetly, that you're taken by surprise by its disturbing imagery and left shaken by the horror and inhumanity it poetically portrays. It is something not so much heard as experienced."* (July 6, 2000).

Reactions were intense. The audience would sit in stunned silence, and finally, sigh. They would sigh before applauding. Reactions varied, but the woman who insisted Billie never sing the song again was unusual. She followed Lady Day into the powder room, then chased her out again. The manager tried to calm her down, and he got her story. At seven or eight years old she had actually witnessed a lynching. A mob tied a black man by the throat to the fender of a car, dragged him through the streets, then hung his body on a tree and burned it. She had completely forgotten the entire traumatic scene, until the song by the Jewish high school teacher, sung by the black blues singer, brought it all back.

It brings it all back—that's what it does. The horror. It is, in that sense, a horrible song. It brings it all back, to all of us. For all of us to remember. *Strange Fruit...*

Can't We Be Friends?

Kay Swift

Who hasn't felt the dread of one of those awful conversations, about "us"? The one where your true love says

Now it seems, this is how the story ends,
he's gonna look at me and say,
Can't we be friends?

"Can't we be friends?" earned its place as a timeless standard, not only due to a fun tune that works in a variety of tempos, but primarily because this is a song that nails a feeling. It freezes that heart-sick moment and describes it perfectly. The words lend themselves to a sentimental ballad or blues, while the perky tune hints of hope. Somehow the combination comforts with empathy and promise.

Maybe there is more to this oddly winsome combination than meets the eye; perhaps lyricist Paul James was secretly hoping for that very conversation to occur—between his wife, composer Kay Swift, and her lover, none other than George Gershwin. Could that be the source of the smile that lurks beneath the anguish of "Can't we be friends?"

It's a long story.

Kay Swift began life as a brilliant, beautiful ingénue. She played classical piano in solo and trio settings so well that she was awarded a scholarship to a fine music college which went on to become Julliard. The sorrow of her early life came when, as a teenage girl, she lost her father, whom she adored,. She never fully recovered from her loss.

At a socialite party in her native Manhattan, she met the illustrious George Gershwin. They seemed to connect on so many levels, the chemistry was irresistible. Gershwin was known to be a "womanizer" but the relationship he shared with Kay Swift would change his life as well. Her depth of musical knowledge enabled her to keep up with, or at least understand his fiery genius in a way that no other lover would. Of course, there was the problem of her husband. James Paul Warburg was a polite, well connected banker on Wall Street. He was a "good choice" and they had married well, if young. Warburg knew he was obviously no competition to the extroverted, gifted star who now pursued his wife.

Gershwin loved to share his talents and his opportunities. From hogging the piano all night at a party to training and encouraging fledgling composers as a mentor, he gave all he could of himself, in his unique way. When he got Kay a job as rehearsal pianist for his 1927 show, it was not to further their affair, it was to launch her career.

She learned from the master, and learned well. She started to write. Her husband stood by her through all this and even tried to help. In an effort to stay with the changes his wife was making, he took to writing some words for the songs she produced. At first it was just a show of support, but as the team kept growing and writing, it did appear that the sedate banker was emerging as a lyricist of talent and originality himself.

It is considered unseemly for Wall Street bankers to write show tunes. And this situation was complicated enough without inviting public scrutiny. So as the songs began to publish, Warburg adopted a pseudonym, simply reversing his first and middle name to become Paul James.

In the midst of the mess came the masterpiece. Nomadic Gershwin was drifting away from his talented lover. Kay found herself discovering new interest in her multi-talented banker. Warburg felt his stock rising. When she brought a bouncy new tune, with undeniable swing to her lyricist husband, he found the vehicle to frame the parting conversation which all the players knew to be coming. Conceptually it made no sense to Kay Swift to take her most upbeat melody and add a maudlin lyric about the end of a love affair—this is the stuff of ballads. Emotionally it was wrenching to watch her husband turn a witty, rhymed phrase about her world famous lover suggesting they become friends. And yet, she could not deny the magic of the musical pairing. As words and melody came together they knew they had a lovable song.

"Can't We Be Friends?" was introduced in 1929 by Libby Holman in the hit review *The Little Show,* and became an immediate hit. Its fortunes rose as America's fortunes collapsed into the Great Depression which began in October of that year. Gershwin moved on, following the music business to California, following his heart to new loves. The team of Kay Swift and Paul James cemented their partnership and wrote hits like "Can This Be Love?" and the title song for their show *Fine and Dandy.*

Gershwin and Swift found it difficult to let go of their love, however. Kay's marriage finally ended, and Gershwin wrote that he planned to return from Hollywood to be with her again. Sadly, he died at age 39 before he could fulfill his promise. Following his death Kay worked with Ira Gershwin in completing George's unpublished and unfinished songs, some of which appeared in the 1947 movie, *The Shocking Miss Pilgrim.*

Later, Kay Swift would go on to serve as the Musical Director for the 1939 World's Fair in New York. After divorcing James, she eventually married a real cowboy and retired to life on a ranch in Bend, Oregon. Her memoir, <u>Who Could Ask for Anything More</u>, was published in 1943 and filmed in 1950, starring Irene Dunne as Kay. Throughout her life she continued writing, turning in two new tunes for a celebration of her work held in her eighty-ninth year! But her lasting contribution will always be the ambivalent bouncing ballad, "Can't We Be Friends?"

Blue Moon

Rodgers and Hart

Jean Harlow was not exactly a singer. In the 1933 movie, *Hollywood Party*, she struggled with a Rodgers and Hart song called "Prayer" (also tentatively titled "Make Me a Star"). She sang it so poorly the producers cut the song, the scene and the singer. Rodgers and Hart were hot in Hollywood just then, and they were not about to throw away a perfectly good song, just because Jean Harlow couldn't sing it! After Larry Hart rewrote the lyric, it showed up as "The Bad in Every Man" in MGM's *Manhattan Melodrama*.

Well, it almost showed up. You can hear a chorus or two, softly sung in the background by lounge singer Shirley Ross in a Cotton Club scene, while William Powell and Myrna Loy rudely outtalk the tune. This gangster movie achieved immortality when it drew Public Enemy #1 John Dillinger to Chicago's Biograph Theater. Leaving the picture house, the infamous mobster was cut down by the Tommy guns of Melvin Purvis and his G-men. But nobody remembered "The Bad in Every Man." So the indomitable team tried again.

Jack Robbins wanted to publish a Rodgers and Hart hit. He liked Rodger's melody, so he urged another rewrite. Larry Hart went back to work. This time he worked around images of loneliness and hope, *"Blue moon, you saw me standing alone...Without a dream in my heart."*

This version made its way, in 1935, into an unnoticed MGM B movie: *The Night is Young*. Once again it languished in obscurity. But when Glen Gray and the Casa Loma Orchestra recorded it the following year, it topped the charts. "Blue Moon" enjoyed three weeks at #1 with Glen Gray's version. Later that year, Benny Goodman took a version of the tune to #2 for a few weeks.

The plaintive ballad appeared in at least half a dozen more movies, notably, *With a Song in My Heart,* and regularly showed up on the Hit Parade. Mel Torme's 1949 version was one of his bigger hits. By the '50s music was changing. "Blue Moon" seemed to change with it. For some unknown reason the King himself cut a version; when Elvis Presley recorded Rodgers and Hart's *Blue Moon,* prim Richard Rodgers was stunned! But nothing could prepare him for the Marcels.

A doo-wop group ("doo-wop," where words or syllables are rhythmically chanted to support a soloist) from Pittsburgh, fronted by Cornelius Harp, the Marcels were students in Oliver Allegheny High School. Jules Kruspir decided to manage them, and got them into Colpix Records. They could only record during down time, when the studio was not booked. One night Kruspir asked for a version of "Heart and Soul." No one knew the song. But "Blue Moon" had the same basic chord pattern, the doo-wop standard I - VI - IV - V. Why not try that? Fred Johnson thought the bass line from the Cadillacs' song *Zoom* would work, so off he went, with "Bomp Boppa Bomp, ba dang ge dang dang." A hit was born!

Two weeks after that recording date, Murray the K, legendary New York DJ, played the demo twenty six times during one four-hour show. On April 3, 1961, "Blue Moon" took over for Elvis at #1. After three weeks at #1 on the rock 'n' roll charts, the doo-wop Broadway ballad became a hit in England, Spain, Japan, and all over South America. The high school group appeared with Chubby Checker and sang "Blue Moon" in the movie *Twist Around the Clock.* It shows up regularly in television shows and movies to this day.

No one has made a serious recording of "Blue Moon" since the doo-wop version redefined the song (with the exception of Bob Dylan's strange 1970 release on his album, *Self Portrait*). It may be the anthem of doo-wop, perhaps the most familiar, recognizable song of that distinct and highly stylized genre. So something's gained and something's lost, as Joni Mitchell might say. An odd fate for the ballad Larry Hart wrote three times, and the simple melody and chord pattern Richard Rodgers utilized; the tune that Harlow couldn't sing—the lonesome prayer to the moon above to send someone to love—exiled to the tundra of doo-wop? They might have to say, 'It never entered our minds."

It's De-Lovely

Cole Porter

Following the dismal failure of Cole Porter's first Broadway outing, *See America First,* Mr. Porter fled the social life he so adored, to join the Foreign Legion in France. Well...actually there was a good year and a half of parties and plays and hi-life at the Yale Club before Porter left for France. His venture to France did correspond with the outbreak of war, and with the possible threat of a draft. Once his age group (that being either 24 or 26, depending) was draft eligible, the peripatetic Mr. Porter felt the urge to visit Paris. The Legion? Oh, that was just thrown in for a little color. Actually, for his wartime service, he volunteered as personal secretary to the President of the Duryea Relief Party, a very social-oriented fund raising effort. He was occasionally seen in French Army uniforms, once as a corporal, again as a Captain, though no record exists of him serving in the French Army. His claims of wartime service, and of receiving the *Croix de Guerre,* then, seem a bit exaggerated—but it was all in fun!

Cole Porter was a wonderfully enigmatic, complicated personality. His life is covered in the chapter on *Night and Day.* His tendency to stretch the truth or to downright lie for the fun of it might have made his personality seem even more enigmatic. His classic hit *It's De-Lovely* from *Red, Hot and Blue!* has several founders, and each comes with an intriguing story.

Moss Hart and Cole Porter collaborated on the play, *Jubilee.* Hart had always wanted to travel the world, so, at Porter's suggestion, they worked on their play while sailing round the world on the *Franconia.* Joined by Porter's friend since college days, the director-turned-actor Monty Woolley, the three arrived in Java. There they sampled a mangosteen melon. Hart went first, "It's delightful!" Porter added,

"It's delicious!" So, naturally, Monty chimed, "It's de-lovely!" The phrase stuck in Cole's mind.

Or no—wait! They were in Rio de Janeiro, Monty and Cole and Linda, Cole's wife. That was it, yes, it was sunrise, overlooking the city of Rio nestled beneath the cliffs, on the beach. As the three friends took in the sight, Cole sighed, "It's delightful." Linda exclaimed, "It's delicious." And Monty, of course, got his line, "It's de-lovely!"

With this clear origin firmly established, Cole set to work. He drafted a version of the song for his movie, *Born to Dance.* MGM didn't like it. So it simmered a while. When the producers of *Red, Hot and Blue!* needed a number to summarize the years of love between Bob Hope and Ethel Merman (Cole's favorite star), he wrapped the story of their first kiss, their engagement, their honeymoon, and their firstborn around good old Monty's—or somebody's—quip: "It's De-lovely!"

The song was an immediate hit. While the play itself met with mixed reviews, the cast and the score were enough to insure a successful run. But *It's De-lovely* became a standard in the repertoire of the nightspots almost overnight. Into the 1950s, singers like Mabel Mercer and Sara Vaughan scored hits with it. While the tune is clever, it is clearly a vehicle. Porter did most of his writing and all of his conceiving away from the piano. The song really had been born in a conversational exchange, and it retained its character throughout. It's delicious, it's delectable, it's delirious, it's dilemma, it's delimit, it's deluxe! It's about the words! It is the fully developed Cole Porter wit, doing what he does best. It's de-lovely!

Quiet Nights of Quiet Stars
Antonio Carlos Jobim and
Gene Lees

The back of a bus in Brazil is a far cry from quiet nights or quiet stars...but what does that matter in the romance of song writing? Why shouldn't a chaotic, State Department sponsored sweep of South America by the Paul Winter Sextet produce a Bossa standard?

In June of 1962 (winter in South America) the State Department did indeed send Paul Winter's Sextet across South America, in what was to be an historic good will tour. Charlie Byrd and Gerry Mulligan were already under the influence, then Dizzy Gillespie and his piano player, Lalo Schifrin began introducing the Bossa beat to their act. The Bossa Nova (the new beat) was set to become the newest trend in popular jazz. In fact, it was to prove to be the final serious bid that Jazz would proffer for the ear of popular music. Rock 'n' Roll was gaining fast.

The new beat from Brazil slid the cool school into many of the sounds we now know as cocktail jazz. It was smooth, sophisticated, and under-arranged. It was this simplistic arrangement as well as the syncopated rhythms that made it unique. Jazz had splintered into several schools. Esoteric, *avant garde* exercises took be-bop to technical heights which most listeners found hard to understand. So the Cool Jazz of Miles Davis, and West Coast Jazz from Brubeck, Chet Baker, Stan Getz et al, offered an understated alternative. And then there was the lush, over-arranged music of vocalists such as Perry Como and the later Nat King Cole, under the baton of Nelson Riddle or his imitators. In the middle of this spectrum, small groups like Paul Desmond's quartets and Winter's sextets held their ground, and searched for new ideas.

Enter the Bossa Nova. Antonio Carlos Jobim was the premier Brazilian composer. He wrote on a nylon stringed guitar, tuned to all fourths, using unique voicings and rhythms. Charlie Byrd picked up on this and brought it home to America. His guitar will forever be linked to the Bossa Nova. Stan Getz found his saxophone voice, and linked his destiny to that of the Bossa. Astrud Gilberto became the foremost vocalist, singing in Portuguese and English, the lyrics of quiet nights, and boys from Ipanema.

And there's the problem. That is where we came in, back on that bus leaving Rio. Jazz journalist, editor and musician Gene Lees was tagging along with the Sextet on their State Department tour. He met Jobim, and the two formed an enduring friendship, in spite of the obvious language barrier—Jobim spoke very little English, while Lees' Portuguese was even worse. They found French, which they both knew sparsely, their best *lingua franca*. So it was in this triangulated milieu of tongues that the task fell to Lees of translating the lyrics of Jobim's songs into English.

Before the band left Rio de Janeiro, Gene Lees had successfully transliterated the tongue-in-cheek "Desafinado" from the Portuguese, retaining enough of the wit to satisfy Jobim. Lees' lyrics, penned in the back seat of a taxi, grasped the subject and worked with the meter. His confidence piqued, Lees next went to work on the thoughtful Jobim composition, "Corcovado." He writes:

> "Corcovado" became "Quiet Nights of Quiet Stars"
> on a bus as Paul Winter and the group and I headed
> for Bello Horizonte. I mailed the lyrics back to Jobim.

"Quiet Nights of Quiet Stars" would go on to carve a niche as the theme song, along with "The Boy (Girl) from Ipanema," of the Bossa Nova movement. As the Bossa frenzy ebbed, "Quiet Nights" emerged as a standard of the jazz repertoire. Recorded by too many instrumentalists to list, interpreted in various styles, whenever the song is sung—in English—it all goes back to the noisy bus rumbling out of Rio on a winter's morning. And, of course, a few quiet nights of quiet stars as well.

Aha! The Moment of

Inspiration

Plato spoke of the artist's *Divine Madness.* Mihaly Csikszentmihalyi wrote of <u>Flow: The Psychology of Optimal Experience</u>. In the twenty-five hundred years separating the two, we have never stopped talking about it. It is that magical moment, the feeling of being "possessed!" The muses, the supernatural forces of beauty, art and music capture us, and reveal themselves. In an instant, we hear the melody, catch the concept, dream the solution. Somehow we reach beyond ourselves, and when we return bearing gifts, we know that they are not of our own creation.

Edison's old adage may well be true: "Genius is 10% inspiration and 90% perspiration." But thank God for the ten percent! These writers and composers knew the perspiration side of the equation well enough—they toiled and tore with the best of them. But they also knew enough to recognize the moment of inspiration when it came.

Maybe they believed in the muses a bit more than the average person. Or maybe they had come to believe in themselves, to see the possibility that they might be able to write a song, or capture a fragment of the celestial melody? Most of them learned to never be far from pen and paper, just in case. They are the ones whose songs live on.

It Had to Be You

Isham Jones

The Jones family was doing very well in 1923. The Depression had not yet begun to suck the blood out of the entertainment industry. Chicago was a Jazz Mecca, and Isham Jones was one of Chicago's finest band leaders. They lived in a nice apartment near the Hotel Sherman's College Inn, where Isham's band was a legendary attraction. In addition to his regular gig at the College Inn, Isham toured and recorded. Royalties from his popular records on Brunswick Records subsidized their lifestyle. He was a star. It was a long way from the coal mines.

Isham Jones quite literally began in the coal mines of Michigan. Like his father, he loved to the play the fiddle; like his father before him, he went into the mines. He ended up leading a team of blinded mules, hauling coal up out of the bowels of the earth. The work was dirty, dark, depressing and dangerous. Black lung disease plagued the miners. Cave-ins threatened lives daily. Isham hated the mines, and loved music. He kept his mind busy during the boring work day by working on musical arrangements or inventing new tunes, playing violin there in the coal mines. One day he led a blind mule right into a closed door, while singing one of his tunes. His foreman suggested he find a new way to keep his mind busy. For Isham the choice between a life in the mines or a life in music was easy. He never went back to the "worthless pit."

He is best remembered, of course, as a composer. His first published title appeared in 1906, *Midsummer Evenings*. But he was also a horn man, a singer, and a piano player. He worked his way across America in the days of touring regional bands. He put together his own orchestra after composing and recording a few hits like

"That's Jaz!," "Oh! Min!" and "Indigo Blues." After a stint in the WW I army, he played saxophone with the "Isham Jones Rainbo Orchestra"—they played the new "Jass" music. He was an early partner in the Brunswick Recording Company when they were still called "Talking Machines." In New York he played on 54th Street. They played a regular night club gig, toured through the Midwest, and recorded with most of the singers on the Brunswick label, including Al Jolson.

Those were the "Golden Days of Jazz." There is something to the sentimental nomenclature. In the "Roaring Twenties" America had money to spend, and loved entertainment. Scott and Zelda weren't the only ones looking for a good party. And there were no D.J.s, there were no juke boxes, radio was a novelty for home use. There was only live music. So every city had its 52nd Street, its Indiana Avenue, its Strip, its Downtown. Any good jazz musician could blow into town and get work. For this rare window in time, the demand for live music was greater than the supply. Kansas City had its distinct sound. New Orleans music spread across the country, permeating its odd rhythms into the Jazz culture.

Cincinnati and Indianapolis, even the small town of Richmond, IN, spawned recording studios and made stars out of locals like Hoagy Carmichael. But Chicago was the Midwest magnet. Like New York on the East Coast, it had everything, a huge and diverse population, mobsters, musical geniuses, a distinct sound, and national radio broadcast. Isham was the toast of Chicago...the Jones family was doing well.

January 31 was Isham's birthday. His wife went all out. She knew they could afford an extravagant gift, and she knew how much he would love a new piano. Their apartment sported a beat up old spinet, which Isham played with diligence. But for his stature, for his professional development, surely he should have a fine new piano.

She completely surprised him. He finished work at the hotel, went out for a few birthday drinks, and arrived home after 2:00 in the morning. There he found his wife waiting up, sitting on a beautiful new piano bench, in front of a beautiful new piano. Isham's joy was unfeigned. He was genuinely surprised, and delighted. So much so, that he stayed up until after sunrise, playing his new birthday piano.

By the time he crawled into bed that morning he had written three new tunes. All of them are still in circulation today, nearly seventy-five years later. "Spain" and "The One I Love Belongs to Somebody Else" were popular. But one has become a true standard, played and recorded over and over. The song "It Had to Be You" was written that cold January night in Chicago, on Isham's brand new birthday piano. When Gus Kahn added the lyrics, a star was born. Royalties from "It Had to Be You" paid for that piano many times over, and helped the family survive the Depression that decimated so much of that nostalgic Golden Age. You might think of this story the next time you find yourself looking for "A gift that keeps on giving."

Yesterday

Paul McCartney

Sometimes song writing becomes supernatural. The muses seem to take over the life of a human being and he or she becomes a vessel of divinity. Mythology gives us good categories for this phenomenon, as we still find ourselves calling on the muses in groping to describe a phenomenon like Wolfgang Mozart or the overpowering charisma of a band like the Beatles. In fact, that may be the best explanation for the audience ecstasy the press of the '60s called Beatlemania.

The screaming teenagers, the fainting girls, the jelly beans tossed onto the stage. They knew they were in the presence of something—transcendent. That is why the music became so important to a generation, it wasn't just music. It was no longer a pretty tune with a good beat and interesting lyrics, "I'd give it about a 78, Dick..." It was a quasi-religious experience.

It can be a dangerous thing to give your life over to the muses, to the archetypes. Marilyn Monroe became the mythic essence of the "Girl with the Golden Hair." She lost her soul, and she lost her life. Many of the great rockers died young, as had the jazz age innovators of a generation before. Kennedy evoked the myth of Camelot, and was struck down before the eyes of America. It sounds flaky, scary perhaps to speak of archetypes or muses in history. But the words themselves betray our deepest knowledge: muse, muses, music.

Consider the case of Paul McCartney. He was just a bass player in a rock and roll band. He sang and played guitar, then moved to bass when they needed a bass player. He couldn't read music, he knew little to nothing about musical history or theory. But as the band evolved, he and his writing mate John Lennon found themselves writing brilliant melodies, haunting lyrics, and so alive with charisma on the stage that they finally had to give up performing because the mob hysteria made it impossible. How can anyone explain this rock and roll bassman writing the melody to "Michelle," or the plaintive "Fool on a Hill"?

The best example of transcendent genius may be the writing of "Yesterday." This standard is the most recorded song in music history; that is to say, more artists have recorded more versions of "Yesterday" than any other song. And it all began with *Scrambled Eggs*.

McCartney tells the story. He woke up one morning with a melody in his head. It seemed to linger from a dream he was having. Dah — da-da. He went for some breakfast, and the melody stayed with him. He experimented with sticking words into the tune, to help him remember it. So he sang "scrambled eggs" while making his breakfast. By the time breakfast was complete, much of the menu had been crammed into the melodic structure that we know today as "Yesterday."

It took another stroke of genius to take that three syllable measure, a half note followed by two quarters, and fill it with the word, "Yesterday." In that one word Paul manages to evoke such a wistful longing for all that once was, and now can never be. It was an era of lost innocence, lost leaders, lost vision, lost hope. It was an age of lost love. It was the quintessential heart break lyric, all that emotion, in a word, and a tune: "Yesterday."

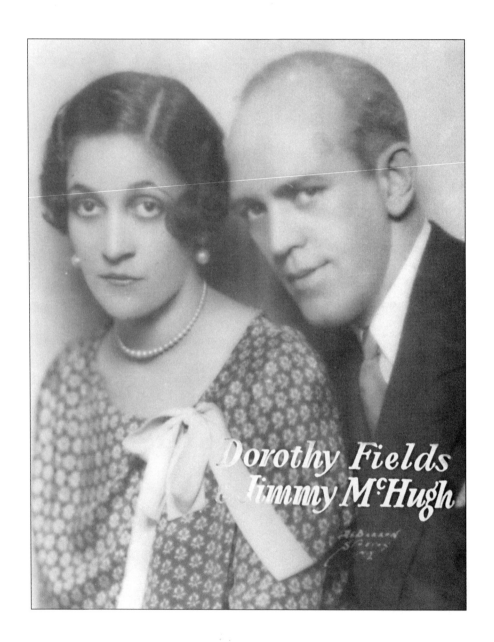

I Can't Give You Anything But

Love
Dorothy Fields and
Jimmy McHugh

Window shopping...that's all they were doing. Gazing at jewelry on display in a Manhattan storefront window. Times were hard for the young black couple as they looked through the glass into another world. Diamonds glittered, mounted in shining silver; rubies and emeralds surrounded the centerpiece, while golden bracelets framed the spectacle. Another woman stopped to look at the jewels, and the couple prepared to move on. Pausing for one more gaze, the man said to his wife, with rueful humor, "I can't give you anything but love, baby." They walked off down the Manhattan streets.

The woman who had momentarily joined them in their window shopping was Dorothy Fields, and the phrase she heard that evening rang in her imagination. Dorothy grew up the daughter of Broadway song man Lew Fields. The family was on intimate terms with songsters like Rodgers and Hart, who wrote for Lew's shows. Dorothy knew she wanted to work in the family business; she wanted to write music. But even with a nice network in place, and all the contacts any aspiring writer could hope for, she still had to write something—something with magic, a song that could become a hit. While she waited to her inspiration, she finished school, she found employment teaching drama. (What else?) She entered into a very unhappy, doomed marriage with Dr. Jack Wiener, and contributed light verse to a small magazine.

In an otherwise insignificant partnership with songwriter Fred Coots, she managed to write a few tunes. Although her lyrics were, in her own estimation, "poor" and nothing was published, the experience convinced her that this was to be her future. She met Jimmy McHugh at Mills Music, and began to write lyrics for his tunes. The team was commissioned to write some new songs for a Cotton Club floor show. It was Dorothy's big chance!

Opening night at the Cotton Club: Dorothy is in the audience with her entire family, beaming with pride. Dorothy was a relatively proper young woman, and cringed with outrage and embarrassment when the sultry singer of her big song began to substitute risqué lyrics for the words Dorothy had worked so hard to perfect. The practice was not unusual; witness Ella Fitzgerald's famous rewrite of "Bewitched, Bothered and Bewildered," but the evening was a disappointment, and something of an embarrassment for her and her family, and Dorothy's big break seemed as far away as ever.

But the team of Field's and McHugh still had the Cotton Club commission, there were more songs to be written. With the phrase from the window shopping couple reverberating through her mind, she began to sketch a lyric.

> I'd like to see you looking swell, baby,
> But diamond bracelets Woolworth's doesn't sell, baby..."

She ran her idea past Jimmy McHugh, and "I Can't Give You Anything but Love" was off—and limping. The song flopped at the Cotton Club. But a Broadway Review, *Lew Leslie's Blackbirds of 1928*, picked up the number. Starring Bill 'Bojangles' Robinson and Adelaide Hall, the show ran for over 500 performances, and the song was a showstopper. Cliff 'Ukelele Ike' Edwards recorded it and it became a huge hit. Like all the standards, it was performed, recorded, sung, talked about, and lived by succeeding generations. It told a story, it captured a feeling that everyone going through the Great Depression knew well. Although the song never referred to the black couple at the storefront, it was their story. It was our story as well.

My Heart Stood Still
Rodgers and Hart

My Heart Stood Still, one of Rodgers and Hart's most enduring hits, boasts a distinctly dramatic genesis. This baby was born in a taxi-cab. In Paris. Stodgy Richard Rodgers and his bon vivant partner Larry Hart found themselves in the back of a Paris taxi with two new "lady friends" (don't tell Dorothy Rodgers!) when the cab narrowly missed a collision. The cabbie was only mildly disturbed—just another day. But in the back seat, Hart's date for the evening cried out, "My heart stood still!" Hart seized the expression, and mentioned to Rodgers that it might make a good song title. Rodgers methodically pulled out his trusty little song notebook and made the entry. Back in London, the girls forgotten, the taxi cab forgotten, the song forgotten, Larry Hart was handed a melody. His partner had a draft for him to work on, a sketch for their song, "My Heart Stood Still." Hart went to work.

It was the spring of 1927. Rodgers and Hart were in London working on the production of a show to be titled, *One Damn Thing after Another.* Jessie Matthews, only seventeen years old, was slated to star in the play. Rodgers described her as a "very young, bright-eyed and toothy doll." At the new show's first rehearsal, Matthews was taught the love song, and dutifully sang it. Producer Charles Cochran immediately recognized a hit, but worried that it had no introduction, no "verse." Larry Hart sprang up from the back of the theater, where he had been chewing on a cigar, and ran down the aisle bubbling, "You want a verse?" He scribbled some lines on a envelope, and handed them to Matthews, "How d'ya like this, babe? Think you can read my writing?"

The show opened on May 19, 1927. The Prince of Wales (later King Edward VIII) was so taken with "My Heart Stood Still" that he declared it his favorite fox-trot. When he requested the song at a subsequent social gathering, the orchestra leader was clueless, so the prince proceeded to teach it—line by line. The incident made headlines, the song took off, and the show was a hit.

The song made its way to Broadway in a new show. Back home in New York, Rodgers and Hart went to work with Herbert Fields (brother to songstress Dorothy Fields) and his father, producer Lew Fields, to set Mark Twain's *A Connecticut Yankee in King Arthur's Court* to music. A prologue was devised to establish the characters, during which Martin and Alice sing "My Heart Stood Still" to one another, before Martin's fiancée catches on and brains him with a bottle, sending him into A D. 528. With a cast of 42, an 18-piece orchestra, and choreography by a young newcomer named Busby Berkeley, *A Connecticut Yankee* scored another Rodgers and Hart smash, and "My Heart Stood Still" won a new audience.

"My Heart Stood Still" began its life as a typical song of the 1920s. But like many of Rodgers' melodies it transcended the genre. Early recordings, such as Jessie Matthews' 1927 version, or that of pianist Edythe Baker, are clearly dated. But through the '30s it smoothed out, subtly changing style with the times. By the 1950s the song was a standard every bit as hip and contemporary as anything being written. Perry Como recorded it twice, once in 1952, and again in 1987. Tony Bennett, Frank Sinatra, Sara Vaughan, Bing Crosby, Bill Evans, Don Goldie, even Diana Ross and The Supremes all took their turn with "My Heart Stood Still"—the song born in the back of a Paris taxi. A chance expression from an unknown lady of the Parisian night. Wouldn't she be proud!

Personalities
Eccentrics Anonymous

Robert Louis Stevenson said:

> *"To be what we are, and become what we are
> capable of becoming is the only creed of life."*

These are the stories of the characters. We have to laugh at the eccentricities of Cole Porter, even as we stand in awe of his achievement. We simply must be amazed at the power, vulnerability and the sheer genius of Billie Holiday, in the middle of the ransacked life she pursued with such energy.

These are the legends. They became what they were capable of becoming. They burned with a flame so bright, that we tell their tales today. They were shocking and they were subtle. They were shy and they were audacious. These composers and lyricists are each unique. They lived into their gifts, with incredible vitality. And they grew into the stuff of legend.

Rabbi Zushya used to teach:

> *"When I go to meet the great creator, I shall not be asked:*
> *"Why were you not Moses?"*
> *I shall be asked,*
> *"Why were you not Zushya?"*

God Bless the Child
Billie Holiday

Billie Holiday was larger than life. She was a walking phenomenon, at least when she was able to walk. Her lifestyle makes Mick Jagger look like a choir boy. Her flame burned so brightly, she lived so intensely, it is remarkable that she lasted as long as she did. It was only her energy that kept her going. More than one friend has reflected that Lady Day had "the most addictive personality in the world." She seemed to hate everything she loved, and love all she hated. But that personal force that drove her so made her one of the unforgettable talents of Jazz.

Eleanora Harris (born February 14, 1915) grew up in the brothels of Baltimore. She was probably a prostitute by nine or ten years old. She loved the blues and barrel house rags in the joints where drinks were cheap and sex was sold. Young Eleanora was nine years old when she was sent by the state to the House of Good Shepherd for Colored Girls. She was there for only a year, but biographers agree that she learned the pleasures of lesbian love there in this all-girl environment, a legacy which she carried through her life. She rejoined her mother, Sadie, at the age of eleven, and the two remained close until her mother's death many years later. She sang along to Bessie Smith on the Victrola. She sang in local bars and clubs. She headed for Harlem at thirteen, and sang her way to fame. She was only seventeen when the roving young impresario John Hammond "discovered" Lady Day.

As a musical star, she was altogether unique. Tough talking, foul mouthed, gun toting, masochistic, voracious for any and every experience, Billie Holiday would magically step out of the violent, chaotic life she led when she took the stage. There she transformed into a charming, astute musician and entertainer. Her musical instincts were uncanny. Her timing has never been emulated. She seemed to sing like a clarinet. Band members describe her as "thinking like a horn player." Listening to her plaintive, nasal tone today, it is easier to hear Benny Goodman than, say, Ella Fitzgerald.

But off stage, life was hard for Billie Holiday. She became the star she never dreamt of becoming. But Lady Day had her demons. She drank constantly, in great quantities. She became a heroin addict. Her lusts were furious, rampant. She might have a date one evening after a show, with her gentleman waiting for her, then notice a few cute show girls in her audience, and leave with the women for a night of pleasure. "Call me later, honey."

Her work habits were notorious. Club owners would only put up with her late arrivals and drunken performances because she was such a draw. Her name out front guaranteed a packed house. She attracted a steady string of abusive boyfriend/managers who beat her and stole from her. She claimed to need the beatings. She fought back as well.

Billie Holiday was tough! She once caught up with a man in an alley in Harlem who had ripped her off on a drug deal. She left her escorts at the entry. She beat the man senseless and then returned to the party. She sent her boyfriends to the emergency room with head injuries from lamps; she cut them with her knives and they returned the favor. As her career careened, she became so self destructive it was impossible to work with her. She might show up two hours late for a 9:00 show, then take an hour in her dressing room, and then start drinking with guests once she hit the club floor. She literally insisted on being punched, kicked and beaten by her manager before she took the stage. She sang with cracked ribs, with black eyes, and she sang with such heart, the audience had to love her!

Lady Day was larger than life.

Songs associated with Billie Holiday include "Strange Fruit," "Lover Man" and "God Bless the Child." She rarely wrote any songs. She might catch a melody and sing it to a collaborator, or perhaps suggest a lyrical phrase or two. The exception seems to be "God Bless the Child."

During the famous ASCAP strike of 1940, nearly all the current jazz standards and pop hits were banned from airplay. Musicians were eager to record new material in hopes of moving in on the open airwaves. Arthur Herzog was a friend, one of the many musicians that worked with Billie. He was looking for a song, something catchy, something with a lyrical line about it. He was with Lady Day, scrounging for ideas. After coming up empty, she began to talk about her mother, Sadie. Seems Sadie wanted money again. This time she wanted Billie to loan her the money to start her own speak-easy, after-hours joint. Billie didn't have it, and even if she did have it, she didn't want to give it to Sadie. She muttered, "Well, you know, God bless the child..."

"What do you mean?" Herzog asked.

"The old saying, you know, 'Momma may have money, Pappa may have it, Cousin's got money, but if you ain't got it yourself, then—God bless the child that's got his own.'"

"That's it!" Herzog sang. He grabbed Danny Mendelsohn, and the three of them spent a half an hour, penning the great torch song of Billie Holiday's career. The song was recorded on May 9, 1941, and was a hit by October of that year. As one of her last hit recordings, it will always be associated with the legend of Lady Day. God bless her.

Night and Day

Cole Porter

Imagine the polar opposite of Billie Holiday. Imagine a white male, born into privilege and wealth, somewhere in the rural Midwest. Make him small, sickly, and exceptionally witty. Now, make him wealthier than you imagined—and even more rural. You are coming close to the legend of Cole Porter.

Peru, Indiana, is somewhere between Fort Wayne and Indianapolis. Today it is a small town, dependent upon a fluctuating agricultural economy. But in the 1890s it was a teeming metropolis of art and culture. Well, no. It was a small Indiana town then, too, in 1891 when Cole Porter was born to his mother, Kate, and father Sam Porter. He derived the name Cole from his mother's family. His grandfather, despotic J. O. Cole, was the scion of the family, and one of the wealthiest men in Indiana in a day of vast personal fortunes. J. O. made his million as a merchant in the California goldrush of 1849. He came home to Indiana to cultivate his investments and his family. His daughter Kate was the apple of his eye, until she married the local druggist, the unassuming Sam Porter. After two children died at birth, little Cole Porter survived to become their only child.

Cole was precocious from the beginning. He studied violin, then quit because he didn't like the noise it made! But even as a little tyke, he was writing piano music, which his mother was able to have published in Chicago. Manuscripts exist today of ten-year-old Cole's *Song of the Birds*. As was customary among families of means, Cole went "out East" to study. He attended Worcester Academy (where he graduated Class Valedictorian), and Yale University. At Yale he made lifelong friends such as actor/director Monty Woolley, and discovered a prodigious talent for mixing popular melodies with clever lyrics. He wrote school plays and football songs, achieved enormous popularity (he was a cheerleader for the football squad) and posted mediocre grades. Less than a semester into Grandfather J. O.'s mandatory law school at Harvard, Cole was writing for Yale Alumni smokers. One thing led to another...

Porter's personality was unique. He spent hours a day on his appearance, including manicures, facial treatments, etc. His dress was extravagant, odd and "dapper." He married into the wealthiest echelons of high society with his marriage to Linda Lee Thomas. They lived in palaces in Venice, traveled the globe incessantly, maintained a vast suite at the Waldorf, a country villa in Massachusetts, and a mansion in Hollywood. The marriage was, alas, sexless. For whatever reasons, Cole's sexuality expressed itself primarily in an attraction to rugged, burly, muscular men, whom he often paid to please him. It seemed to remain a separate and distinct orbit in his personality constellation, light years away from the urbane, cheerful persona he presented. But his parties were famous for every type of indulgence, in a social circle of the very indulged indeed.

Through the last golden days of Broadway in the pre-Depression '20s, into New York and Hollywood of the '30s, on into the war years and beyond, Cole Porter shared top honors only with Irving Berlin. His shows/films include *Gay Divorce*, (Movie: *The Gay Divorcee*), *Anything Goes, Born to Dance, Kiss Me Kate,* and *High Society.* The list of hit songs written by Cole Porter is staggering. "Night and Day," "Miss Otis Regrets," "I Get a Kick Out of You," "Anything Goes," "You're the Top," "Let's Do It, Let's Fall in Love," "Don't Fence Me In" (yup, that's a fact, pardner, the Roy Rogers song!), "Begin the Beguine," "Just One of Those Things," "I've Got You Under My Skin," "Be a Clown," "My Heart Belongs to Daddy," "I Love Paris," ...well, you get the idea.

When tragedy struck, the vain and infamously self-indulgent Mr. Porter showed a remarkable fortitude. He was forty-five years old, and looked at least ten years younger. He was famous, wealthy and successful beyond his wildest dreams. But it was all changed by a horse. In a strange riding accident, the experienced equestrian Porter took a fall that crushed both his legs. For the rest of his life he struggled with braces, canes and wheelchairs. He was often carried from room to room, endured thirty-five operations, lived in constant

pain—often wracking pain, and with the ever-present threat of
amputation. Yet the songs that flowed from his pen remained, for the
most part, witty, fun and filled with *joie de vivre*. Embroidered on the
pillows that covered the couches of his New York apartment was a
motto: *"Never Explain; Never Complain."*

His ethic he summarized as "Play and Work." For Cole it was
both, all the time. He collaborated with Moss Hart on a show, *Jubilee,*
while cruising around the world. He never began a tune on the piano,
preferring to work out the basic rhymes and tunes in his head. Later
he would spend the necessary hours at his piano, assembling the
various parts of the song he had conceived in solitude, in travel, in the
festivities of the evening or wherever his fertile mind happened to
roam. We may be tempted to assess his genius primarily a lyricist, as
we read a delightful lyric like:

> *In olden days a glimpse of stocking,*
> *Was looked on as something shocking,*
> *But now, God knows,*
> *Anything Goes!*
> *Good authors too, who once knew better words,*
> *Now only use four letter words,*
> *Writing prose,*
> *Anything Goes!*

But then we notice how we are humming the tune; just how
inseparable the words and melody have become. We think of all the
instrumental versions of Cole Porter songs we have heard, and we
admit they cannot be parted, the tune, the lyric, the genius of Cole
Porter.

Consider "Night and Day," one of the most popular and enduring of
Cole Porter's standards. The show, titled *Gay Divorce,* debuted on
November 29, 1932. By then the Depression was well underway, and
Cole's habit of writing about the very affluent upper crust ran the risk of
rubbing America wrong. The show made a laughing stock of divorce
proceedings, among other things. Yes, even in 1932 it had a *double
entendre,* though only for those "on the inside." It ran for 248
performances on Broadway, then crossed the Atlantic for a very successful
run on the London stage. It was a smash. Fred Astaire and Clare Luce
starred, buoyed by the stellar score provided by Cole Porter, featuring

"Night and Day." The song was written specifically with Astaire's limited vocal range in mind. One month following the opening of *Gay Divorce,* "Night and Day" was listed in *Variety* as one of the leaders in record and sheet music sales. The tune drew serious praise from Irving Berlin:

> "I am mad about 'Night and Day,' and think it is your high spot...orchestra leaders think it is the best tune of the year, and I agree with them."

It lasted eighteen weeks on *Variety's* Top Ten list, enjoying five weeks at No. 1. "Night and Day" follows a formula Cole once explained to Richard Rodgers, which Rodgers described in his autobiography. Apparently Cole had shared with Rodgers over dinner that he had noticed that most of the hits were written by Jewish songsmiths, Jerome Kern, Irving Berlin, the Gershwins, so he, the WASP from Indiana, set out to write 'Jewish tunes.'

> "Hum the melody," writes Rodgers years later, "that goes with 'Only you beneath the moon and under the sun' from "Night and Day," or any of "Begin the Beguine," or "Love for Sale," or "My Heart Belongs to Daddy" or "I Love Paris." These minor key melodies are unmistakably eastern Mediterranean."

Was this formula shared with envy, or anti-Semitism? Was Cole teasing Rodgers, himself of Jewish descent? We cannot be sure today, but probably not, asserts Rodgers. Emulation, after all, is the most sincere flattery. The final word on Cole's formula:

> "It is surely one of the ironies of the musical theater that despite the abundance of Jewish composers, the one who has written the most enduring 'Jewish' music should be an Episcopalian millionaire who was born on a farm in Peru, Indiana."   —Richard Rodgers

Since 1932, "Night and Day," the song written for a limited singer with a small vocal range, to a Semitic formula by an Episcopalian from the farm, has never been far from the stage. It has been recorded by virtually every Jazz singer of renown. It is one of those songs we all seem to know, somehow. The bar quiets a bit when the singer starts it. You hear Sinatra master the song on your radio as you pull in the garage, and you stay in the car, just to listen. It is, in a word, a Standard.

It Might as Well Be Spring

Richard Rodgers

Richard Rodgers was as paradoxical a personality as any of the flamboyant "Wild Things" who set their lives to the music of Jazz. His Broadway career spanned sixty years; he was seventeen years old when the first melody by Richard Rodgers skipped across the Broadway stage, in 1919. *I Remember Mama,* the last Rodgers musical, opened May 31, 1979. Revivals, movies and recording after recording keep the Rodgers repertoire as current as tomorrow's Top 40. He was not only one of the giants of the musical stage, he was a wonderful song writer. Pick up a "fake book" or "real book" or any collection of Jazz standards, look for Rodgers and Hart, then go on to Rodgers and Hammerstein. Now, here comes the paradox.

Rodgers wrote some of the most romantic music in the repertoire. Sample a few titles: "Isn't it Romantic," "My Romance," "My Funny Valentine," "Some Enchanted Evening," "My Favorite Things," "My Heart Stood Still," "It Might as Well be Spring," "Little Girl Blue," "You Took Advantage of Me," "Blue Moon," "Hello Young Lovers," "You'll Never Walk Alone," "It Never Entered My Mind," "The Lady is a Tramp," "Bewitched," "There's a Small Hotel," "It's Easy to Remember." Richard Rodgers teamed up with lyricist Lorenz Hart and later Oscar Hammerstein II to create incredibly romantic songs. Their appeal goes beyond the lyric; the melodies themselves sing and lilt, suggest and evoke such a mood of romance and love that they are heard behind many romance movies to this day. Yet, you would never suspect it to meet the man. He was a cold, calm business man.

By the peak of his career, when he was producing shows with partner Oscar Hammerstein, Rodgers was usually regarded as an intimidating, controlling perfectionist. He negotiated contracts with a ruthless lack of "romance." Hammerstein had not only graduated from law school, but had been a practicing attorney before turning to song writing for a profession. But he let Rodgers run the business— he was no match for Rodgers' savvy.

That type of personality produces few friends. For eighteen years Rodgers and Hammerstein were the most important, powerful song writing team in the world. Towards the end, as Hammerstein was dying, he said to Stephen Sondheim, "We've worked together all these years, and I don't really know him." But that was by design. They carefully structured their partnership to avoid interpersonal conflict. Rodgers' previous collaboration, with mercurial Larry Hart, had been weighed down with a great deal of personal baggage. Likewise, Rodgers, toward the end of his career, was quoted as saying, "To this day I don't know if he (Hammerstein) really liked me." If he did, he was in a distinct minority. Not very many people liked Richard Rodgers.

He usually wore a blue, pin-striped suit. He sat in at rehearsal and scared the cast. "Here comes Godzilla," a cast member might mutter when Rodgers entered. After the Hammerstein days, Rodgers found it impossible to collaborate. Alliances with Alan Jay Lerner ("He had something in common with Hammerstein and Hart—not liking to work." —Richard Rodgers) and Stephen Sondheim ("They all ended up hating each other." —Rodgers' biographer William G. Hyland) collapsed into battles about egos.

Diahann Carroll summed it up about as kindly as she could:

> "I came to the conclusion that he was really incapable of hearing someone else's point of view without regarding that person as a potential adversary, and his frequent insensitivity was appalling."

And yet! Juxtapose the twin peaks of this paradox and you realize what a huge "and yet" the enigma of Richard Rodgers has become. It is almost as if Rodgers invested every ounce of romance that his soul could muster (Sondheim once described him as being "of infinite talent, but limited soul.") into his music. There was simply no romance, no imagination left for his life. He seemed to function almost as a *savant* of sorts, abounding with love and energy and life in the world of music, while utterly devoid of these qualities in the real world of friends, work, family etc.

One of the most unusual aspects of Rodgers' exceptional talent was the speed and apparent effortlessness with which he wrote. Handed a lyric, he could write a song—perfectly suited, carefully matching in mood and meter—in less than an hour. He never understood how Hart or Hammerstein, let alone Lerner, could spend weeks writing a song. It's only a song—it's business, after all.

When Rodgers and Hammerstein first came to Hollywood, the idea was to follow their great success on Broadway with *Oklahoma!* by remaking the 1933 movie *State Fair*. Jeanne Crain, as Margie, was to open the show in a wonderful, wanderlust mood. Hammerstein needed a song to evoke this spirit and set up the character. He complained to Rodgers that even though State Fairs were never held in springtime, for Margie, "It might as well be spring." Rodgers told his partner he had just named the song. Once Hammerstein's lyrics were presented to him, he knocked out the tune with his customary dispatch.

"It Might as Well Be Spring" entered the line-up with so many other love songs by Richard Rodgers...the prolific romantic, Godzilla, the paradox on Broadway.

Take Five

Paul Desmond and Dave Brubeck

Dave Brubeck almost gave up jazz. It was too much of a hassle. He was the kid, the hick from the sticks. His technique he acquired from his mother—his only piano teacher. His theory he simply heard. No one was playing like Brubeck when he arrived in Stockton, California. He was the cowhand from Ione, a cattle town. Brubeck grew up on a cattle ranch. He works his own ranch today. But back then, when the hip players found out he was from Ione, they walked away. Same deal when he moved from Stockton to Camp Haan.

This time the move came courtesy of Uncle Sam. In an attempt to learn jazz as well as serve his country during the WWII war effort, Brubeck enlisted into the Army Band. Camp Haan then hosted four 28-man bands. Dave was an outcast—until they heard him play. His phrasing, timing and intensity blew away the Army players. No one played like Brubeck!

Some three months into the invasion of Normandy, the Army broke up the bands and turned their musicians into riflemen. Brubeck found himself in France, marching toward Metz, heading for the front. When his division stopped by an Allied base camp, Dave discovered a Red Cross show organizing to entertain the troops. They needed a piano player. Brubeck volunteered just as his division was moving on. Dave Brubeck missed marching into German fire by roughly ten minutes!

After the war the G.I. Bill put Brubeck through Mills College in Oakland, where he studied with his favorite teacher, Darius Milhaud. He planned to become a classical pianist. His jazz was not accepted. His playing was too polyphonic. His timing was too weird. He was sick of all the rejections, the snobbery of his fellow musicians, and the misunderstanding of his message. When Stan Kenton read through one of Brubeck's arrangements, he told the younger musician, "Bring it back in ten years." It isn't easy being ten years ahead of your time, especially if you plan to keep growing and changing. So Brubeck decided to stop growing.

For six months Milhaud and Brubeck talked over the role of Jazz in the culture. It was Milhaud who finally convinced Brubeck to stay with the music he knew and loved. By 1950 Brubeck was writing for Downbeat, teaching at the University of California, recording on the Fantasy and Coronet labels, and playing a regular radio gig, as well as lounge work. In 1951 his trio broke up and Brubeck formed a quartet with saxophonist Paul Desmond.

There was an immediate, strange bond between the two stylists. Brubeck played heavy-handed, chunky chords, with fast runs and polytonal extensions. Desmond, on the other hand, played a gentle, melodic alto. His soft tone sounded a bit like Lester Young. In the heyday of be-bop, Desmond won popular polls with baffling regularity. He was quoted as saying, "I have won several prizes as the world's slowest alto player, as well as a special award in 1961 for quietness." Somehow their counterpoint worked. Paul Desmond and Dave Brubeck would play together until Desmond's unofficial retirement in 1967, and on and off informally until his death from cancer ten years later.

Together Brubeck and Desmond relentlessly pushed the creative envelope. Both were intrigued with time signatures—couldn't something be done to stretch the way music approaches timing? Something beyond the occasional two bar measure in a 4/4 song?

For the concept album *TIME OUT,* they each drafted tunes in non-traditional time. A great deal of collaboration took place between the two (and drummer Joe Morello) when Paul Desmond came back with a rough sketch of *Take Five.* The timing was perfect; it was a foot tapper that anyone could count, but it could challenge the best drummer! 1 -2 -3 -1 -2. Why not? Brubeck suggested reversing the bridge and the verse, the band played through this backwards arrangement—and a hit was born!

Desmond recalls:

> "At the time I really thought it was kind of a throw-
> away. I was ready to trade the entire rights, lifetime-
> wise of 'Take Five' for a used Ronson electric razor.

And the thing that makes "Take Five" work is the bridge, which we almost didn't use. We really came within…I shudder to think how close we came to not using that, because I said 'Well, I got this theme that we could use for a middle part.' And Dave said, 'Well, let's run through it.' And that's what made 'Take Five.'"

For seventeen years the Dave Brubeck Quartet was the most commercially successful combo in jazz. They may still hold the record. Their theme song, of course, was "Take Five." Its irresistible melody and clever timing have made it a perennial favorite in the jazz repertoire. Stan Kenton was correct in telling Brubeck to wait ten years. Eventually culture caught up to the genius of Dave Brubeck, making him a star and "Take Five" a standard.

The Hard Way
The Fight for Love and Glory

Inspiration can come easy. Paul McCartney wakes up one morning and pens "Yesterday" over breakfast...but it isn't always so. The challenges many of these songwriters faced are hard to imagine. Some were born into a luxury and self-indulgence that never should have produced a disciplined genius. Others grew up in the kind of prostitution and drug abuse that routinely, callously crushes the spirits of the young and gifted. Some were immigrants, or the children of immigrants. They had dreams, and they hung on.

Then there are the songs themselves. They, too, faced persecution, censorship and obscurity. "Somewhere Over the Rainbow" was too sad for a children's movie. "Love for Sale" was too racy for Broadway.

Once an African tribesman wanted to give a special gift to a Western visitor. On her birthday he presented her with a beautiful shell. The sea was over fifty miles away. The tribesman had walked the fifty miles to the shore, and brought her seashell the fifty miles back. It was the hundred-mile hike that made the seashell priceless to the Westerner. Her friend explained, "The journey is part of the gift."

Lush Life

Billy Strayhorn

Billy was a small, effeminate, shy teenager, growing up in the toughest part of Pittsburgh. He loved the theater, and knew someday that he would pursue this love. His father was an abusive alcoholic, who seemed to despise his son's artistic nature. His mother understood him, and tried to protect her sensitive son. She had managed to get him the piano that took up so much room in their tiny shotgun house. The poverty joined fist in glove with the prejudice to crush any distant hints of hope: they were a poor black family in a steel town in the depths of the Depression. But Billy had other ideas.

He dreamed, even as a young teenager, of sailing to Paris or joining the sophisticated night life of the nascent Harlem Renaissance. All of that seemed so far away from the steel gray slums of Pittsburgh. But not when he played his music. The music was everything for Billy. It had always been that way. He could carry on a conversation while sketching complex scores for a brass ensemble. He could play anything he heard, by ear, and he could sight-read any score dropped in front of his weak, myopic eyes. So he dreamed of the life he would one day live—a life of debonair society, of ascots and martinis. And he wrote of his dreams.

Billy Strayhorn wrote "Lush Life" at the age of 18. Before he ever left Pittsburgh the song was essentially completed, music and lyrics. In retrospect it is incredibly prophetic: he lived exactly the life the song describes. His heart was set on a life of twelve o'clock tails, of sophistication and self indulgence, of weekends in Paris ending up in "some small dive."

Strayhorn was possessed by an awesome musical genius. It flew forth from him, flawless, triumphant, defiant, robust. It propelled him into the high courts of his time. Within a year after penning "Lush Life," he would be playing it for the Duke. He joined Duke Ellington's entourage at 20. The chord changes to the tune are incredibly complex, moving through key signatures with deceptive fluidity and perfect attitude. Through his career as Ellington's arranger and co-writer, Strayhorn wrote few lyrics, but the words to Lush Life say everything, perfectly. It is almost eerie now to read over this predicted blueprint of the life the young artist was to lead.

Strayhorn knew his destiny, and he pursued it with intensity and abandon. He would become the hard drinking, sophisticated musical companion of Duke Ellington. He was one of the few openly gay black artists of the Harlem Renaissance. His mild manners and diminutive appearance earned him the nickname Swee' Pea among friends like Lena Horne, Leonard Feather and Martin Luther King Jr. A steady smoker, he died of cancer of the esophagus at 51 years old. Friends speculate that his drinking would have taken him if the cancer didn't. He was usually quiet and reserved; as a celebrity he shunned the limelight. He left that for the Duke, much of whose famous music was actually penned by Billy Strayhorn. And all the loneliness, the longing, the excitement and shallowness, the parties and the partings, all of the fame and wealth, successes and sorrows of the life he was to live are captured in the song he wrote at 18.

Actress Diahann Carroll said of Strayhorn, "He was a beautiful, delicate little flower, just, you know, a genius, but a tortured genius. He was an unhappy person. His genius was so overwhelming that being in his presence was something you could never forget."

Sammy Cahn spoke of his and Sinatra's admiration of *Lush Life:* "Frank and I loved that song. Those words, the maturity, sophistication...you really had to have lived a life to write that. Frank adored that." When he was told that Strayhorn wrote the song as a teenager in Pittsburgh, dreaming of a life he had, in fact, not yet lived, Cahn replied, "Then I amend my words, which I rarely do, by the way. He wasn't only talented. He had some balls."

Get Happy

Harold Arlen and Ted Koehler

Harold Arlen got his first real job as a singer in May, 1929. His efforts to break into Vaudeville seemed to be going nowhere, so he answered a casting call. The show was called *Louisville Lou,* a *Showboat* emulator, and 24-year-old Harold got to sing and play piano on stage as "Cokey Joe." The show debuted in Philadelphia to such praise as, "slipshod," "tedious," and "cumbersome." They had a little work to do. The script doctors and choreographers cut and pasted. The show limped to New York, where they opened in Queens, to more disdain and more changes. With his New York band falling apart, the great Fletcher Henderson took work as a rehearsal pianist for the production. Then came the fateful day that Henderson called in sick.

"Cokey Joe" had a small part in the show, now called *Great Day,* and no one bothered rewriting it. Arlen often found himself bored and ignored, surrounded by creative cacophony. Dancers worked on their steps at center stage, while lines were read and rewritten off stage, and songs were tweaked for a chorus in a far corner of the theater. When Henderson took a day off, it gave Arlen a chance to play some new music, as dance accompanist. He played the two-bar pickup on cue, took the dancers through their steps, and cut out every time the choreographer interrupted the dancers. Then he fiddled softly with the pickup until it was time to cue the girls again. He was passing time, hardly even improvising consciously, just playing around. First one of the girls asked him, "What is that you're playing?"

Howard Warren, a seasoned Tin Pan Alley song plugger and writer, noticed the dancers huddled around the piano; he came over for a listen. He asked the same question, and got the same answer,

"Nothing—just fooling around." But the dancers liked it. And Warren liked it!

"You got a song there, kid, and I know the guy to write the lyric." Nothing to lose, Arlen thought as he agreed to meet "the guy." Warren set the meeting at the office of his publishing company, Remick, in mid-town Manhattan. Ted Koehler was ten years older than Arlen, and at 34 was a well established lyricist. It had not been an easy journey for him. He had worked in his father's shop doing photoengraving all day. By night he played the hot joints across the river in Newark, where he lived with this family. His father finally issued the ultimatum: give up the late nights and the jazz crowd; take his job more seriously, or move out of home and find a new job. Koehler chose the latter, and never looked back. He played piano for vaudeville stars like Rudolph Valentino (the film career was in a slump) and Sophie Tucker. He traveled the country. Then he came home to New York, where he joined the Remick Company as a song plugger and staff writer.

He had heard a lot of songs by the time he met this young piano player with one tune he had made up between dance steps. He had every right to be skeptical. Still, it was Harry Warren's recommendation. Tall, shy and immaculate, Harold Arlen was not particularly impressive, until he began to play. Koehler recognized genius when he heard it.

The lyricist asked the young pianist to play his song again—and again. And again. And again. It slowly dawned on Arlen that this was the man at work; this was his new partner, *at work*. Ted lay down on the couch and listened, relaxed but intent. He seemed almost to be sleeping. He was listening.

He started with the odd three-note tag that repeated through the A section. He heard the hints of a "Negro spiritual," he felt a driving rhythm, a mood emerged from the melody, and Koehler offered a three-beat phrase: "Get Happy."

Koehler borrowed heavily on the imagery of the old spirituals to round out the lyric with references to Judgment Day, the Lord, troubles, sins and sinners, and The River. And don't forget "Hallelujah!" The folks at Remick were so impressed with the song that they immediately hired Arlen at $50.00 a week, beginning July 31, 1929, just two months before the crash. He quit his job with *Great Day* and got a new apartment.

The song was interpolated into a 1930 Broadway show, benefiting from a long friendship between Koehler and the show's star, Ruth Etting. For many good reasons, *Ruth Selwyn's Nine-Fifteen Revue* bombed. It bombed even in the dismal climate of Post Black Tuesday Broadway. The Depression would permanently shift the balance of entertainment power, and the great Broadway of the Twenties would be gone forever. Poor *Ruth Selwyn's Nine-Fifteen Revue* lasted for only six shows. In less than one week it was all over—the show, the song. It was Arlen's second experience with disaster in the theater. Then something odd happened. The song didn't go away.

As everything went from bad to worse, as the full impact of the Depression began to be felt, as four million Americans lost their jobs and unemployment doubled in less than a year, "Get Happy" became a hit. Jazz bands played the upbeat song in night clubs across New York and across America. Numerous jazz instrumental versions were recorded.

Despite a few faltering experiments predating "Get Happy," Harold Arlen thinks of it as his first song. Out of this preliminary effort came a well paying job, security through the onslaught of the Depression and a solid reputation as a composer. But the best was yet to come.

Twenty years later Judy Garland reintroduced the song to a new generation in the 1950 film *Summer Stock*. The clip of Garland singing "Get Happy" in the midst of her emotional anguish and physical problems is a masterpiece of vocal interpretation. It is probably this luminescent treatment that secured the song's place in the jazz standard repertoire. Ironically, this was not her first Harold Arlen song. The composer would be destined to write such tunes as "Ding Dong the Witch is Dead," "If I Only had a Brain" and "Somewhere Over the Rainbow" for a younger Judy Garland to sing as Dorothy in *The Wizard of Oz*. But all that lay in the far distant future, for twenty-four-year-old Harold "Cokey Joe" Arlen, and his only song, "Get Happy."

Somewhere Over the Rainbow

Harold Arlen and Yip Harburg

Hyman Arluck was born in Buffalo in 1905. His father was cantor in the local synagogue, and by seven years old, Hyman was singing in the choir. His parents encouraged his musical interests, until he dropped out of high school at age fifteen, to play piano and organ in Buffalo silent movie theaters. From this illustrious beginning he soon was fronting the Snappy Trio in local cafes and eventually sailing Lake Erie with the Southbound Shufflers. Next came a stint as singer, arranger and pianist with the Buffalodians (!) before Hyman decided to change his life and his name and moved to the Big Apple.

Now named Harold Arlen, he hit the city and went to work. In no time he was singing and playing piano with a well known dance band that found their way to the stage. As pianist and pit intermission singer for George White's *Scandals of 1928*, Arlen met Vincent Youmans, who introduced him to Harry Warren, who got him together with lyricist Ted Koehler, and they wrote, for their first song together, "Get Happy." The song debuted in *Ruth Selwyn's Nine-Fifteen Revue*. The Revue faired poorly, but the song became a hit. The team decided to stick together, cut back on performing, and focus on writing songs. They wrote for Broadway and for eight Cotton Club revues between 1930 and 1934. Hits like "I've Got the World on a String" and "Between the Devil and the Deep Blue Sea" followed easily enough, until the team produced the timeless classic, "Stormy Weather." Originally the song was written for Cab Calloway, but when Duke Ellington backed Ethel Waters at the Cotton Club, a true musical event occurred. "Stormy Weather" was a smash. Ten years later Lena Horne sang it in the movie *Cabin in the Sky* and the song found a new audience.

Hollywood came next. He worked for Columbia, Goldwyn and Warner Brothers, and got to know George Gershwin. Partner Ted Koehler went to work as a film producer, so Harold seized the chance to work with a number of lyricists, including Ira Gershwin, Lew Brown and Yip Harburg.

MGM, meanwhile, was in the early stage of developing a unique film, featuring color and black and white, titled *The Wizard of Oz*. The studio engaged songwriting legend Jerome Kern, but before he could get to work on the project he suffered a heart attack and was ordered off work. Arlen was freelancing at the time in Hollywood, so the job fell to him and one of his partners, Yip Harburg. Suddenly Arlen's long time friend and hero George Gershwin succumbed to a brain tumor. Arlen's own health was questionable; he was suffering prolonged headaches. Friends suspected he identified too strongly with Gershwin, but a medical examination found "a cyst of the *maxillary antrum* pressing on a nerve." After surgery, Harold went to work for MGM.

The original deal for MGM to borrow Shirley Temple from Twentieth Century-Fox fell through, and hopes for *The Wizard of Oz* were low. Sixteen-year-old Judy Garland was hired to play the twelve-year-old Dorothy. Her theme song, "Somewhere Over the Rainbow" came easily to Arlen; he loved the melody from its birth, but it was an uphill climb from there.

Lyricist Yip Harburg found it too sophisticated a tune for a twelve-year-old to sing. He didn't like the melody at all, but Arlen stuck by it. Yip tried to "dumb the song down" with childish images and language. Arlen pushed for the intelligent and poignant lyric. At the film's first preview for the MGM executives, they suggested cutting the song from the movie, insisting it "slowed down the action in the first part of the picture."

Through Arlen's tenacity and Judy Garland's charmed rendition, "Somewhere Over the Rainbow" made it through the cutting room and into America, where it met with a heartfelt welcome. Harold Arlen would be nominated for nine Academy Awards, but his only Oscar win was for "Somewhere Over the Rainbow." That year *Your Hit Parade* featured Judy Garland's "Somewhere Over the Rainbow" as the number one radio hit for seven weeks.

Arlen went on to work with Johnny Mercer to pen many more beloved standards, such as "That Old Black Magic," "Blues in the

Night" and "One for My Baby and One More for the Road." Together they wrote "Ac-cent-tchu-ate the Positive" and many more familiar tunes. Later Arlen teamed up with Ira Gershwin for the film *A Star is Born,* and wrote, among others, "The Man that Got Away" (once again for Judy Garland). But nothing would ever match the haunting beauty of "Somewhere Over the Rainbow."

Judy Garland once told an interviewer, "I have sung it hundreds of times, and it's still the song that is closest to my heart. It is so symbolic of everybody's dream and wish that I am sure that's why people sometimes get tears in their eyes when they hear it... It is very gratifying to have a song that is more or less known as my song, or my theme song, and to have had it written by the fantastic Howard Arlen."

Love for Sale

Cole Porter

Cole Porter was known for his risque lyrics. Songs like "Sweet Nudity" or "Back to Nature with You" regularly fell out of his fertile imagination. Sometimes they were called for, as in an entire show about a young English schoolgirl determined to lose her virginity: *Nymph Errant.* Often they were just for fun. Porter's wit drew from his own "liberated" lifestyle and seemed to parody every type of experience or desire. Through the 1930s theatergoers of New York and London, joined later by movie and record/radio audiences, would snicker to wry descriptions of cocaine use:

> Some they may go for cocaine;
> I'm sure that if, I took even one sniff
> It would bore me terrifically too
> But I get a kick out of you.

But one time even Cole Porter went too far. The song was titled "Love for Sale," from the show, *The New Yorkers.*

In this uncomfortably explicit lyric we find none of the characteristic *double entendres,* and so little of the humor we come to expect from the droll Cole Porter. Read here, without the accompanying tune, it captures a haunting, melancholy description of tragic advertising for a young prostitute. Cynical and sad,

> *Let the poets pipe of love in their childish way,*

our young streetwalker ends her number with a clever but clear invitation:

> *If you want to buy my wares,*
> *Follow me and climb the stairs.*

Cole Porter's urbane lifestyle was nearly as celebrated as his talent. He lived the life he so often sang about. He dined on caviar, he rented palaces, he maintained a twelve room suite in New York at the Waldorf-Astoria, he traveled the world, frequenting Paris and London, hiking Macchu-Piccu for something interesting and different. (See the chapter on *Night and Day* for a more detailed description of Porter's biography.) But there was a shadow side to the glamorous life of wealth and privilege. His sexual drive was dark and insatiable. He could spend $2000 for one night of pleasure with a male prostitute. That is, of course, two thousand 1933 dollars, during the height of the Depression!

While he enjoyed an occasional long term relationship with a male lover/friend now and again, there was always the drive for anonymous, rough sex for money. He designed a couch specifically for these adventures, his "fucking couch." He was drawn to the waterfront, to the seamiest bars, to the kind of places where the sophisticated Mr. Cole Porter would never be seen. His sexuality had become a sort of alternative to the rest of his life. It represented a shadow, something completely apart from all the rest of his polished and perfected persona. They struck their balance, these two lives. He had accepted himself, enjoyed the admiration of his friends, and earned the respect of the professional world. But he never wrote from this secret self. Except once.

The song was just too much. Even for Broadway. Even for Cole Porter. *The New Yorkers* opened on December 8, 1930. Newspaper and radio denounced the song as "in the poorest taste." "Love for Sale" was banned from radio play. Recorded by Fred Waring and his Pennsylvanians (they were featured in the Broadway production, in their New York debut) the song, of course, became an instant hit. With rumors flying, it was soon in the floor shows of most New York night spots. The producers had a hit (168 performances) show, with a hit song. But they risked the wrath of censorship. The show could be closed down if public outrage demanded it. The solution they hit upon, from today's perspective, seems far more scandalous than the song itself.

As the play was initially written and staged, May (played by Kathryn Crawford) sang the tune, with three sister streetwalkers on back-up vocals. Ms. Crawford was white. Responding immediately to the threat of public disapprobation, producer E. Ray Goetz and staff adroitly rearranged the casting. Now the song was set in Harlem's famed Cotton Club, and sung by a black ingénue. There! The problem was solved. No one in 1930 seemed to mind an African American woman selling love. The show was saved, and the song went on.

"Love for Sale" finds an easy place in today's repertoire. It is still a sad song, with its minor key melody and plaintive lyric. Today, songs about prostitution seem as common as lyrics telling us to kill cops or have indiscriminate sex. Yet today, the racist stereotyping implicit in the production adjustments would provide an absolute scandal. And Cole Porter would savor the irony!

Torch Songs

"And now, ladies and gentlemen, we'd like to slow things down a little bit...and do a song about a feeling. I guess it's a feeling that all of us have known. There's something sweet, something comforting in the song about a broken heart. It's almost like we can share the loneliness, and maybe, somehow we find a friend there. Maybe we feel understood, or a little less lonely, or maybe we just feel gooooodd!"

Nancy (with the laughing face)

Phil Silvers,
Jimmy Van Heusen and
Frank Sinatra

In 1944 Phil Silvers was a comedian. Frank Sinatra was a singing sensation. Jimmy Van Heusen was just a songwriter. In a unique and confusing way, the combination came up with "Nancy (with the laughing face)." Van Heusen wrote the tune, after Silvers dropped off the lyric. It was to be a surprise for Frank and little Nancy, his daughter, a four year birthday present, in fact. The idea came from conversations Sinatra had with Silvers.

They had been on tour together, so Sinatra and Silvers spent many long hours together. Frank Sinatra was a wonderfully complex character with ample assessments and biographies, but he evidently did not like to be alone. After a show he often drank and relaxed with his comrades. In 1944-45, his comrades included Phil Silvers. Sinatra did not make a USO tour until after the European War ended, but he did go over in May, 1945, crossing the Atlantic with Silvers and the whole cast. By November of that year, "Nancy (with the laughing face)" was hot.

It was probably before the crossing that Sinatra had shared his lonely longing for his three-year-old daughter with the comedian...perhaps in those wee small hours of the morning talks that flow out of the artificial intimacy of exhaustion and collaboration. The relationship back home in Hoboken with his wife was tumultuous and complicated. But little Nancy, missing her Daddy, was perfect for sentimentality and imagination—the stuff of romance!

Traveling the country, then during the long and boring ocean crossing, the images came together. The song credits Phil Silvers with the lyric, but the emotion belongs to Dad. And while Sinatra wrote few lyrics, Phil Silvers wrote even fewer.

Sinatra came home from Europe. His musings were presented to him and his daughter for her birthday as a complete song, with music by the veteran composer Van Heusen. Frank loved the tune, for obvious reasons. He recorded it in the studio, but it was never released. However, a version of the tune did make it onto V-disk, a government authorized recording for military use. Played over armed forces radio, just following Sinatra's tour, the song became an Army favorite, a song about life back home, a song about loneliness and the longing for home and family.

When the troops came home they wanted to hear "Nancy (with the laughing face)." Another version was recorded and released, and went to the *Billboard* top ten. Sinatra's career would plummet from this high point. Shortly after the war the big band became a thing of the past. For a variety of reasons, swing music gave way to the popular "crooners" like Nat Cole or Perry Como, and eventually, rock and roll. Most of the big band singers faded away, while a few went to Hollywood, like Doris Day, and found new careers as movie stars.

Sinatra would slump for several years, then determinedly come back with his part as Maggio in *From Here to Eternity*. He would re-invent himself several more times over the course of a legendary career that spanned some seven decades. He became an American Icon.

His daughter Nancy would go on to pursue her own career. She never became an icon, but she had her moment of fame with "These Boots are Made for Walking." And she sang "Something Stupid" with her Dad. She became a celebrity in her own derivative way, one of the first offspring of famous parents to go for stardom herself. By now Nancy Sinatra in her go-go boots presents a nostalgic glimpse of a bygone era. But in one song, for four minutes, any four minutes we want, little Nancy is just turning four, and Daddy is coming home. Frank is a loving Dad, longing for his happy home and his sweet, affectionate daughter. It's all the way it's supposed to be. "Nancy (with the laughing face)."

The Way You Look Tonight
Jerome Kern and Dorothy Fields

By the middle of her career Dorothy Fields had arrived. She
overcame the embarrassment of her beginnings at the Cotton Club.
After her hit "I Can't Give You Anything But Love," she had gone on
to triumph with an upbeat answer to the Depression's theme song of
"Buddy Can You Spare a Dime," penning with partner, Jimmy
McHugh, the lovable "On the Sunny Side of the Street." When the
pair moved to Hollywood together in 1935, they created the perennial
standard, "I'm in the Mood for Love." (Louis Armstrong took it to
Number One.) When Jimmy McHugh went back to New York she
found herself in Hollywood, with most of the finest songwriters of her
time. Then she got the opportunity of a lifetime.

R.K.O. Studios had purchased *Roberta,* a mediocre Broadway
show with some wonderful tunes. But the songs needed a bit of
rewriting, to fit the Hollywood styles, and to fit into the scenes in the
picture. Pandro Berman, the twenty-nine year old genius head of
production, lined up Fred Astaire and Ginger Rogers, handsome
Randolph Scott, and talented (and lovely) Irene Dunne to star. But
the biggest name associated with *Roberta* belonged to the composers.
Oscar Hammerstein wrote the lyrics, with music by Jerome Kern.

Jerome Kern, by 1935, was also known as God. With P. G.
Wodehouse and Guy Bolton he had virtually invented the musical
play and an integrated production. Musical theater had been largely
reviews and comedies with unrelated songs interjected for
entertainment prior to these three penning the famed Princess
Musicals. Then, in 1927, he and Oscar Hammerstein had written
Showboat. Archivist Miles Krueger wrote, "The history of American
Musical Theatre, quite simply, is divided into eras: everything before

Showboat and everything after *Showboat.*" Richard Rodgers and George Gershwin are among the immortals who learned at the feet of Jerome Kern.

Roberta was just another show to Kern. But for Dorothy Fields, it meant a chance to work with God. Hammerstein had left for New York and other projects, with Kern to follow. The studio needed some brush-up lyrics, and had Kern write a new 16-bar song for a scene in the movie featuring models on a runway. The 16 bars made it an unorthodox tune (most songs then, as now, fell into a 32-bar pattern). Then the studio added a typical lyrical stipulation—it had to work as love song in addition to a fashion show. Kern did not know Dorothy Fields, except, perhaps, by reputation. But back in 1904 her father, Lew Fields, had given him a break, back when Jerome Kern was just a struggling song peddler, so he approved the selection of Lew's daughter Dorothy to pen a few lyrics for the show.

The largesse of the great man continued. Kern had left for New York when Dorothy brought her completed 16-bar love ballad, "Lovely to Look At." Producer Berman loved it, and he used it. They shot the scene, using the music, with no approval from God. When Kern saw it he also loved it. And he loved Dorothy. They went on to work together for numerous projects. First there was that song to add into the show; Kern and Hammerstein had written "I Won't Dance" for an ill- fated Broadway bomb, *Three Sisters.* With enough rewriting, the song could be inserted into *Roberta.* While the original Hammerstein version can still be heard now and then, the Kern-Hammerstein-Fields version of "I Won't Dance" went straight to Number One, and today is a recurring favorite, in the repertoire of most of the great jazz interpreters. Dorothy and Jerry (God) formed a lasting friendship. Kern loved to joke, and Dorothy loved to laugh. She was a frequent houseguest and became one of the "three Dorothys," along with Dorothy Hammerstein and Dorothy Kern.

The team's greatest collaboration came, perhaps, with the song "The Way You Look Tonight." It was one of several hits written for the 1936 R.K.O. Astaire/Rogers picture, *Swing Time.* The film is an absolute classic, containing "I Won't Dance," "Pick Yourself Up," "A Fine Romance," "Bojangles of Harlem," and, of course, "The Way You Look Tonight." Dorothy loved to tell the story of the songs creation. For the first time in their partnership, she had handed Jerry

Kern completed words to two songs before he wrote a note ("A Fine Romance" and "Pick Yourself Up"). But "The Way You Look Tonight" started with a melody. An experienced musician with ten years of penning hits under her belt, Dorothy tells the story:

"The first time Jerry played that melody for me I had to leave the room because I started to cry. The release absolutely killed me. I couldn't stop, it was so beautiful."

Others reacted with equal passion. Cabaret star Mary Cleere Haran calls it the most beautiful song ever written. The Motion Picture Academy concurred, awarding Kern and thirty-year-old Fields their Oscar for best song in 1936. Since 1936, "The Way You Look Tonight" keeps popping up. It appears in movies, in instrumental versions, and in countless vocal covers. What do you think of, when you hear those first few lines?

Someday, when I'm awfully low,
When the world is cold,
I will feel a glow just thinking of you,
And the way you look tonight.

Biography

About the Author:

Dr. Chuck Denison is a writer, speaker, consultant and musician. During the day he works for the Presbyterian Church USA designing new models of ministry. As a jazz musician, he has played at the Indy Jazz Fest and many other venues. He has also been a poet, blues guitarist, merchant marine, cab driver, pastor, songwriter and folksinger. Those were the fun jobs. He lives in Louisville KY with his wife Cindy.

About the Photographer:

Duncan Schiedt has photographed jazz musicians for sixty years. He is the author of several books, including The Jazz State of Indiana and Twelve Lives in Jazz, and is co-author of "Ain't Misbehavin". Schiedt's original and archival photographs were featured in Ken Burn's landmark PBS series Jazz, and his work has appeared in international art exhibits and trade and academic publications worldwide. His latest book is titled Jazz in Black & White.